# TABLE OF CONTENTS

Unless otherwise indicated, all Scripture quotations are taken from the King
James Version of the Bible.
*The Uncommon Leader*
ISBN10: 1-56394-154-6 / ISBN 13: 978-1-56394-154-2 / B-106
Copyright © 2006 by *MIKE MURDOCK*
All publishing rights belong exclusively to Wisdom International
Publisher/Editor:  Deborah Murdock Johnson
Published by The Wisdom Center · 4051 Denton Hwy. · Ft. Worth, Texas 76117
1-817-759-BOOK · 1-817-759-2665 · 1-817-759-0300
**MikeMurdockBooks.com**

Winners Are
Simply Ex-Losers
Who Got Mad.

-MIKE MURDOCK

# WHY I WROTE THIS BOOK

I love to see people *succeed* with their life.

God, the Creator, does too.

As the artist treasures his painting and the master craftsman the quality of the violin he created, so our Maker cherishes the dreams, goals, excellence of life, and the happiness you and I are to enjoy.

Through searching diligently for principles for successful living, I became aware of these *two forces:* the *Person* of Jesus and the *Principles* He set in motion.

The Person of Jesus Creates Your Peace.

The Principles of Jesus Create Your Prosperity.

The Person of Jesus Prepares You For Eternity.

The Principles of Jesus Prepare You For Earth.

*Winners Are Simply Ex-Losers Who Got Mad.* They got tired of failure. *The Day You Get Angry At Your Failure Is The Day You Start Winning.* Winning does not start *around* you...it begins *inside* you.

Happiness begins between your ears. Your mind is the Drawing Room for your future experiences. *What Happens In Your Mind Will Happen In Time.*

Mind-management should be the first focus for Overcomers. "Whatsoever things are true, whatsoever things are honest, whatsoever things are just, whatsoever things are pure, whatsoever things are lovely, whatsoever things are of good report; if there be any virtue, and if there be any praise, think on these things," (Philippians 4:8).

The *system* I discovered in The Bible *worked!* It

has multiplied my joy by increasing my ability to succeed a thousand times over. The Master Keys found in this book contain the Wisdom you need to succeed.

Circle today's date on your calendar. Declare that the happiest and most productive days of your life are beginning *today!* Never, never, *never* quit. You may be *minutes* from your miracle.

I wrote this book for *you.*

I pray that each page will give the *added edge* you need to make your life happier, more fulfilling, and to help you become the Uncommon Leader God created you to be.

Mark pages important to you. Use highlighters to remind you of special keys that help you. Read every page carefully.

*The Difference In People Is Who They Have Chosen To Believe.*

> Dr. Mike Murdock
> The Wisdom Center
> 4051 Denton Hwy.
> Ft. Worth, Texas 76117
> MikeMurdockBooks.com

P. S. You may email me personally at... DrMurdock@TheWisdomCenter.tv.

# ∾ 1 ∾

# DISTINGUISH BETWEEN WHAT MATTERS MOST AND WHAT MATTERS LEAST

*Develop Decisiveness.*
Few people are.

Have you ever noticed the hesitation in drivers at a four-way stop? I have seen people sit for 30 seconds at a four-way stop waiting for everyone else to make the first move! I have sat at restaurants with people who could not decide in 20 minutes what food they wanted to eat! Some have even asked the waitress what she thought they should eat!

*Decisiveness can be cultivated.* Think about what you want. Give it *thought.* Invest the Seed of time. *Contemplate.* Meditate on it.

What do you want to be happening in the circle of your life 10 years from today? What are the *ideal* circumstances for your retirement? *What do you dream of becoming?* Do you have a personal list of goals and dreams? Have you taken the time to write them out in detail?

## *Assess Your Home Environment Again*

Several years ago a brilliant young lady suggested that I take a tape recorder, walk into each room of my home and describe clearly what I wished that room to look like. Something wonderful happened! I described exactly how many pens and pencils I wanted, the kind of paper I wanted beside the telephone, and so forth. It became detailed, energizing and thrilling!

Few people have taken the time to find out what really *excites, energizes* and *motivates* them personally.

Something interesting happened in my personal meditation time some weeks ago. I had been a little concerned that my interests frequently changed. For example, the colors my decorator would select for my home would be exciting and thrilling to me. I felt that I would never want to change my mind about them for years to come. A few weeks later, I discovered another combination of colors that excited me *again*. Obviously, I did not feel comfortable about suddenly changing everything that had been done in my home, nor did I really have the finances to do so. I bought a car. I loved it...for about 3 weeks. Then, I was bored and wanted a change.

I felt impressed of The Holy Spirit to begin to write down a list of things that had never changed inside me over many years. It was quite a list of interesting things...and it really put my mind at ease that there was more stability within me than I realized. Many things have never changed what-soever within me, such as my love for information, my desire to collect books and my excitement over receiving a rare new coin from a friend. Another thing that had never changed was my continual need to change my environment. Regardless of how beautifully my bedroom or kitchen was decorated...

within 12 months or so, I was tired of it. That has been a consistent trait.

*Some things never change about you.* What are they? Put down this book for about 15 minutes. Take a sheet of paper, and as quickly and thoroughly as possible, begin to document the things about yourself that have been pretty consistent over the years. Go ahead. Do it now. (Example: Have you always loved books? Animals? Talking?)

Now, after you have done this, you will begin to get a fairly accurate and specific photograph of certain things that you want in your life, around you *daily*. You will also get an awareness of the *quality* of life you are struggling to experience.

## Ask More Questions About Your New Needs

Some years ago, I asked a consultant to come into my offices for several days. He was to discuss any complaints or ideas with each member of my staff. Then I wanted him to compile a report, unbiased and unprejudiced, as to what he thought about our ministry organization. He interrogated me and questioned me for hours. He would take long walks with me and ride in the car; even while I was in crusades, we would talk on the phone. His constant questioning sharpened my focus remarkably. I have never forgotten the experience.

He was relentless in collecting data about my personal needs, desires and appetites toward life. When were the *happiest* moments of my life? What days did I seem to enjoy life *more* than usual? What were the 3 biggest problems I thought about the most…every day? Who were the people that were stressful for me to be around? Who were the people in whose presence I was the most relaxed? How did I want to be remembered? What did I consider to be the most important task that I did each day, each week, each month? If I had to eliminate 50 percent of my entire ministry workload, *what would I delete?* If I were to have a sudden health crisis, experience a heart attack or some other medical emergency, what would I change *first* about my *daily lifestyle?*

Riveting questions were hurled at me continually. Slowly, but surely, a remarkable understanding of what I *really* wanted out of life developed.

Here is a marvelous little exercise. It could change your life forever. Ask one or two of your closest friends, who are skilled at analyzing and dissecting situations, to interrogate you—quizzing you relentlessly, extracting information from you until you have a perfect and complete photograph of the invisible future you are laboring to bring to reality. Something is driving you…pushing you toward your future. What *is* the invisible dream you are subconsciously trying to birth within you and your life?

## *Decisiveness Is Magnetic*

Decisiveness is the catalyst for the aura that surrounds extraordinary and unforgettable people. They simply know *exactly* what they want.

When you are sitting in a restaurant sometime, do a little test. Carefully observe the entry of customers. Notice those who saunter and amble in as if they are not quite certain they have chosen the right restaurant. They slowly walk to their seats wondering if they should even stay at the restaurant, and are unsure about which table to select. Then, observe carefully those who stride in confidently and with a firm, clear and raised voice, express to the hostess of the restaurant, "Good evening! We need a table for 4...by the window, if possible!" Notice how the hostess responds quickly, with enthusiasm and immediately begins to communicate to the other workers exactly what was requested.

When ordering your own meal at a restaurant, *speak up.* Speak firmly. Do not mumble.

Someone has said, "If you will raise your voice 10 percent and walk 20 percent faster, you will generate remarkable new energy, compelling others to respond favorably to you, thus raising the level of self-confidence in every single person around you."

Scriptures command us to avoid indecisiveness. "But let him ask in faith, nothing wavering. For he that wavereth is like a wave of the sea driven with the wind and tossed. For let not that man think that he shall receive any thing of the Lord. A double minded man is unstable in all his ways," (James 1:6-8).

## *What Is Causing Your Indecision?*

What happens when you are totally undecided about an issue or decision? There is a reason for it. The reason may be lack of *sufficient* information...it may be lack of *accurate* information. When this happens, simply declare with great decisiveness, "I have decided to wait 90 days until additional information arrives." You have retained the climate of confidence and decisiveness. *Make decisions clearly.*

Notice Ruth said it quite clearly, "Whither thou goest, I will go; and where thou lodgest, I will lodge," (Ruth 1:16).

*She knew what she wanted.* She *communicated* to Naomi what she wanted. She was *bold* about what she wanted.

## 7 Decisions That Can Change Your World In 7 Days

1. **Decide Who You Will Ignore.**
2. **Decide Who You Enjoy.**
3. **Decide Who You Want To Impress Most.**
4. **Decide Who Has Ignored You.**
5. **Decide The Tasks You No Longer Enjoy Doing.**
6. **Decide Whose Example Is Worth Following With Passion.**
7. **Decide What You Want Your Daily World To Be Like.**

*Continuously Distinguish Between What Matters Most And What Matters Least.*

This is One of the Secrets to becoming an Uncommon Leader.

# ☙ 2 ☙

# RISE ABOVE THE STIGMA OF ANY QUESTIONABLE EVENTS OF YOUR PAST

━━━►❧•◦•❧◄━━━

*Your Past Is Over.*

*Focusing On Your Future Masters Your Past.* "Brethren, I count not myself to have apprehended: but this one thing I do, forgetting those things which are behind, and reaching forth unto those things which are before, I press toward the mark for the prize of the high calling of God in Christ Jesus," (Philippians 3:13-14).

Are you having self-doubts today? Your limited education...your father dying when you were young... an alcoholic parent...guilt over a serious mistake you made in your teenage years? These thoughts are common. It is very important that you remember your past is over.

## *Jesus Never Discussed The Turbulence of His Early Years*

Jesus was born with a terrible stigma. His mother Mary, was pregnant with Him before she ever married Joseph. The Bible says they had not had a sexual relationship. "That which is conceived in her is of the Holy Ghost," (Matthew 1:20).

Only two people in the world really knew that Mary was a virgin...*God* and *Mary*.

Undoubtedly, hundreds of people mocked and sneered at Joseph for marrying Mary.

Jesus grew up with this stigma. He stepped out of a cesspool of human scorn. He clawed His way out of a pit of questions. He ignored the slanderous remarks. He knew the truth. He knew who He was and what He was about. It did not matter that others did not believe. *He chose to chart His own course.* The opinions of others did not matter.

*He never looked back.* He never discussed the situation with anyone. There is not a single Scripture in the Bible where He ever brought up His background or His limitations.

## *Let Yesterday Die*

You too, can move beyond the scars of yesterday. Stop talking about your limited education. Quit complaining that everyone in your family is poor. Stop repeating stories of those you have failed. Stop pointing your finger at the company. Stop advertising your pain. Stop meditating on your flaws. Everyone has limitations. Each of us is handicapped in some way...physically, emotionally, mentally or spiritually.

Concentrate on your *future*. *Rise Above The Stigma of Any Questionable Events of Your Past.*

This is One of the Secrets to becoming an Uncommon Leader.

# ❧ **3** ❧

# PRACTICE THE DAILY HABIT OF SELF-TALK

*What Consumes You?*

*You Will Only Succeed With Something That Consumes You.* Significant leaders build their daily agenda around their Assignment. Their schedule and their plan is totally focused on the completion of their Assignment. Their library is filled with books about their Assignment. Their best friends are those who *celebrate* (not tolerate) their Assignment.

When you hear the name, Thomas Edison...you think, *inventions.* When you hear the name, Oral Roberts...you think, *healing.* When you hear the name, Henry Ford...you think, *automobile.* When you hear the name, Michael Jordan...you think, *basketball.*

*You Will Only Be Remembered For Your Obsession.* It may be a good obsession or an evil obsession. Whether you are Billy Graham or Adolph Hitler...you will be known for one thing...*what consumes you, your mind and your time.*

Ruth would not even pursue the normal path of dating others. She built her lifestyle around the survival of Naomi. *She never considered an option.*

It may be your personal business. It may be the spiritual life of your children. *You will almost always succeed with anything that has the ability to demand your total focus and attention.*

Joshua called it, "not looking to the right or to the left." Others call it being "single-minded." James said, "A double minded man is unstable in all his ways," (James 1:8).

*She refused to consider any alternatives to her Assignment.* Ruth would not go back to her in-laws. She refused to return to the village of her youth. She had developed *total focus* on her Assignment.

*The Only Reason Men Fail Is Broken Focus.* If you fail in life, it will be because something was introduced to you as an option...an alternative to what God told you to do with your life...and you *accepted* it.

Consider Moses. The Bible says, "When he was come to years, refused to be called the son of Pharaoh's daughter; Choosing rather to suffer affliction with the people of God, than to enjoy the pleasures of sin for a season; Esteeming the reproach of Christ greater riches than the treasures in Egypt: for he had respect unto the recompence of the reward," (Hebrews 11:24-26).

*There is no Plan B for your life.* There is only one plan...one *Master Plan* of the Creator Who made you. *Consider nothing else as an option.*

This is what made Ruth an unforgettable woman.

As Naomi walked with her two daughters-in-law, Orpah and Ruth, she turned and said, "Go, return each to her mother's house: the Lord deal kindly with you, as ye have dealt with the dead, and with me. The Lord grant you that ye may find rest, each of you in the house of her husband. Then she kissed them; and they lifted up their voice, and wept," (Ruth 1:8-9). She kissed them. They wept.

Both said, "We will return with thee unto thy people."

Naomi instructed, "Turn again, my daughters: why will ye go with me? are there yet any more sons in my womb, that they may be your husbands? Turn again, my daughters, go your way; for I am too old to have an husband. If I should say, I have hope, if I should have an husband also to night, and should also bear sons," (Ruth 1:11-12).

They lifted up their voice. They wept again.

Orpah left. Yet, Ruth cleaved unto her. Naomi rebukes, "Behold, thy sister in law is gone back unto her people, and unto her gods: return thou after thy sister in law," (Ruth 1:15).

Ruth was *tenacious*.

She was *bold*.

She was *focused*.

Yes, her husband was dead.

Her father-in-law was dead.

Her sister-in-law had returned to her family.

Her mother-in-law was instructing her to return home.

*There was not a single Encourager in her circle.* She did not have *one* single spiritual cheerleader in her life.

She was *alone*.

She was the only one with the desire to pursue a *different* future.

Her Past had no encouraging memories.

Her Present had no encouraging motivation.

Her Future was up to her alone.

*She knew it.* "Intreat me not to leave thee, or to return from following after thee: for whither thou goest, I will go; and where thou lodgest, I will lodge: thy people shall be my people, and thy God my God: Where thou diest, will I die, and there will I be buried: the Lord do so to me, and more also, if ought but death part thee and me," (Ruth 1:16-17).

*She was willing to motivate herself when nobody else was capable or caring.*

Most of us appreciate a lot of encouragement... daily...consistently. It is wonderful when your mate is there to hold your hand through the valleys of uncertainty. It is a precious thing when your little girl looks up and says, "Daddy, you can do anything!"

Your pastor is a gift from the Lord when he looks into your eyes and tells you, "I prayed for you last night, and God spoke to me to reassure you, and tell you that your circumstances are going to change very soon."

## *Do You Really Feel Alone?*

What if there was no one in your life to speak a word to encourage you? *Would you still persist?* Would you stay focused? Would you remain bold and tenacious in your goal and dream...when absolutely nobody really cared?

Ruth did...her tenacity made her an unforget-table woman.

It is what can make you an Uncommon Leader right now.

You see, *every true Leader knows Seasons of Aloneness.* Moses must have known *Seasons of Insignificance* alone in the desert. David must have felt disconnected from the great climate his brothers enjoyed, as they won victory after victory in Saul's army. Certainly, it is wonderful and desirable to have encouragement around you. If you are really going to produce significantly...you must learn the secret of *motivating yourself...encouraging yourself...*accessing the deepest currents within your own heart.

*If you keep waiting for everyone else—you will never move from where you are.*

You can *stay* motivated.

You can *stay* enthusiastic.

You can *stay* energized.

You can motivate yourself *when* you develop a consuming obsession for a specific future you desire.

*Stop* complaining that your mate is not interested in your personal dreams.

*Stop* whining when your children show no interest in your personal goals.

*Stop* holding self-pity parties. Nobody attends them anyhow.

*Embrace your future.* Do it with total abandonment, joy and full excitement that *tomorrow is going to be the best season of your life.*

*Decide The Legacy You Want To Leave.*

*Practice The Daily Habit of Self-Talk.*

This is One of the Secrets to becoming an Uncommon Leader.

RECOMMENDED INVESTMENT:
Seeds of Wisdom on Motivating Yourself, Vol. 31
  (Book/B-171/32 pages)
**Order Online Today..! MikeMurdockBooks.com**

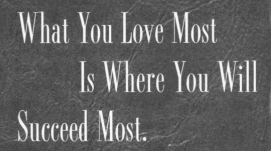

What You Love Most
Is Where You Will
Succeed Most.

-MIKE MURDOCK

# 4

# STAY IN THE CENTER OF WHAT YOU LOVE MOST

*Do What You Do Best.*

**Your Work Should Produce Your Joy.** "And also that every man should eat and drink, and enjoy the good of all his labour, it is the gift of God," (Ecclesiastes 3:13).

*Your Joy Is Determined By Doing What You Love.*

Jesus associated with fishermen. He talked to tax collectors. Doctors and lawyers and religious leaders were regularly in His life, but He never wavered from His focus. The Bible says that "God anointed Jesus of Nazareth with the Holy Ghost and with power: Who went about doing good, and healing all that were oppressed of the devil; for God was with him," (Acts 10:38).

*He knew His mission.*

Some people take jobs because they are convenient or close to their home. One man told me that he had spent his entire life working on a job that made him miserable.

"Why have you worked there for 27 years then?" I asked.

"It is only 10 minutes from my house," he replied. "And in 3 years, I will receive a gold watch. I do not want to leave too early and miss my gold watch."

► What do you love to do?
► What do you love to talk about?
► What would you rather hear about than anything else on earth?
► What would you do with your life if money was not a factor?
► What do you do best of all?

*What you love is a clue to your calling and talent. Stay In The Center of What You Love Most.*

This is One of the Secrets to becoming an Uncommon Leader.

# ∾ 5 ∾

# NEVER MAKE IMPORTANT DECISIONS ALONE

*Learn To Reach.*

It is not a sign of weakness to reach. "Where no counsel is, the people fall: but in the multitude of counsellors there is safety," (Proverbs 11:14).

A famous billionaire of our day was trained by his father. In one of his recent books, he said that he called his father a dozen times a week. He also telephones his own office 12 times a day. He said, "If I do not constantly stay in touch with my business, it's gone." Stay in touch with your supervisor, your boss, or anyone who supervises you, mentors you or is guiding you into something you want to accomplish. Stay in touch *regularly*.

Jesus was brilliant. He was a miracle worker. *He constantly consulted His Heavenly Father.* "Then answered Jesus and said unto them, Verily, verily, I say unto you, The Son can do nothing of Himself, but what He seeth the Father do: for what things soever He doeth, these also doeth the Son likewise," (John 5:19).

*Jesus was open to His Father about His feelings.* In the garden of Gethsemane, He cried, "O My Father, if it be possible, let this cup pass from Me: nevertheless not as I will, but as Thou wilt," (Matthew 26:39).

*Jesus was persistent in pursuing His Father.* "He went away again the second time, and prayed," (Matthew 26:42). Jesus felt alone. He lived in our world. He felt feelings you feel. He is our elder brother, and He was not too proud to reach.

*Know the power of connection.* Create contact. This is the first step toward increase. *Somebody is a link to your future success.* Tomorrow hinges on your ability to pursue them. Do it.

*Never Make Important Decisions Alone.*

This is One of the Secrets to becoming an Uncommon Leader.

### Would You Pray This Prayer Aloud With Me Now?

"Father, give me the intelligence and humility to consult those who are guiding me. Put in me the desire to remain humble and seek after You every day. Father, please keep me from becoming too proud to reach. In Jesus' name. Amen."

# ≋ 6 ≋

# CUSTOMIZE YOUR ENVIRONMENT TO KEEP YOURSELF MOTIVATED

*Atmosphere Matters.*

Invest whatever is necessary to create the atmosphere that motivates you.

*Your chosen focus requires a unique climate.*

Your surroundings are so important. Your atmosphere must receive your attention. It will not happen automatically. You must control the atmosphere around your life or it will control you.

## *14 Facts To Remember About Your Environment*

**1. Your Climate Influences The Decisions You Make.** When you are in a high fashion clothing store, the music is often quiet, classical or dignified. When you go into a store where the younger generation makes purchases, the music is fast, upbeat and energizing. The merchants have created an environment that influences you to buy.

**2. Your Surroundings Contain Colors That Affect You Emotionally.** Many years ago, I read where a certain shade of pink was used in prisons to reduce violence and fights. Some say that bodybuilders can lose one third of their ability if they look at a pink wall while working out. *Colors affect us.*

Colors affect our strength, our enthusiasm and the decisions we make.

**3. Everyone Needs Something Different Around Them.** You must discern what environment and atmosphere brings out the best in you.

When I need energy and I must move quickly from project to project, I love to listen to praise music that is energizing and exciting. When I want to ponder and reflect, I love to listen to slower, more worshipful music. I know the value of protecting the climate around myself.

**4. Nobody Else Can Create Your Atmosphere For You.** You must discern it and pursue it for yourself.

**5. Nobody Else Is Responsible For Providing You With The Climate You Desire.** It is *your* life, *your* needs and *your* decisions.

**6. You Will Not Do Your Very Best Until Everything Around You Is In Place.** Yes, you may achieve and be productive to a degree. However, you can multiply the results of your life when the things around you strengthen and motivate you.

**7. What You See Controls What You Desire.** When you see a billboard advertising hamburgers, you suddenly receive a desire for hamburgers. That is why you must surround yourself with pictures and images of the things you want.

**8. What You Are Viewing Daily Affects What You Desire To Do.** When children see the playground at McDonald's, they are suddenly inspired to stop everything and go play.

**9. Keep Around You Photographs of Things You Want In Your Future.** It may be a boat you want to buy, a home you want to live in or a picture of yourself 20 pounds lighter. These images are influencing the direction your decisions will take you.

**10. Your Environment Is Worth Any Investment In Music And Equipment.** Buy a stereo or whatever it takes...get the best possible.

Every morning, I listen to the Scriptures on my cassette recorder or ipod. That is the first thing I do each day. Yes, equipment costs. My future and my emotions are worth any investment.

I purchase candles that have the best and strongest fragrance and last the longest. Placing them around my room helps provide the most incredible atmosphere of reflection, warmth and caring. *I need that.* My heart requires it. If I do not do it, it will not be done. So, because it is *my* life that is so vital to me, I invest *whatever* is necessary.

A few days ago, I spent over $100 on several CDs. Yet, when I purchased them, I really was not *just* purchasing some music on compact discs. *I was purchasing an atmosphere.*

You see, this morning, after listening to the Bible on tape, I turned the CD player on. On the 6 CDs were birds, a sparkling, flowing fountain and peaceful music. Within seconds, I felt like I was under the trees alone and quiet, tasting the richness of God's nature around me. Yet, I was in my bedroom! I did not have to spend $2,000 to take a vacation to Honolulu. I simply needed an investment in my atmosphere—the appropriate CDs.

**11. Your Investment In Interior Decorating Can Make A Huge Difference In Your Productivity.** A new rug, a picture on the wall, a vase with a rose...every small thing can increase the warmth and caring of your environment.

**12. Invest The Effort And Experimentation To Discover What You Really Need Around You.** This is worthy of your time, too. It is wonderful to explore variations of climates and environments. An interior decorator, the suggestions of a friend or your own personal visits to different stores can help you discover the atmosphere you prefer to work in, play around or simply relax and rest in. Each atmosphere produces a different emotion.

**13. Do Not Wait On Others To Initiate Changes In Your Environment.** Make any investment necessary to create the kind of environment that inspires you toward excellence and the improvement of your life.

**14. Your Atmosphere Can Often Determine Your Productivity.** Many businesses have discovered an increase in unity and employee morale when they played music quietly throughout their offices.

It does not cost a fortune to create a favorable atmosphere. Just think, look around and ask questions. *Explore a little*...experiment.

Invest whatever is necessary to create the atmosphere you want to surround you. *Create The Environment That Keeps You Stimulated.*

*Customize Your Environment To Keep Yourself Motivated.*

This is One of the Secrets to becoming an Uncommon Leader.

RECOMMENDED INVESTMENT:
How To Double Your Productivity In 24 Hours
  (Book/B-137/32 pages)
**Order Online Today..! MikeMurdockBooks.com**

# 7

# MAKE TOMORROW BIGGER THAN YESTERDAY

*Become A "Tomorrow Thinker."*
Ruth created a future far different from her past.
Ruth was a Moabitess girl raised in heathenism. Moab was the son of incest between Lot and his daughter. Ruth married Boaz. God put them together...and ushered in the lineage of Jesus Christ.

Ruth and Boaz produced Obed. Obed produced Jesse. Jesse produced David. David ushered in the lineage of Jesus Christ. *Who was Ruth?*

Ruth was the great-grandmother of David, the greatest warrior Israel has ever known. She was the great-great-grandmother of one of the wisest men who ever lived on earth, Solomon. Through her, and Boaz, came the precious Son of the living God, Jesus of Nazareth.

*God Never Consults Your Past To Decide Your Future.* Satan may remind you of yesterday's mistakes. Do *not* listen to him. *God never reads your diary.* Your past is over. Act like it. Talk like it. Live like it.

Your best days are *ahead* of you.
Your worst days are *behind* you.
There are 3 kinds of people you permit in your life.

*Yesterday, Today And Tomorrow People.*

*Those God Used In Your Life Yesterday May Not Belong In Your Future.* Do not worry about it. Move quickly toward the promises of God. Prepare to enter your future without yesterday people.

You will not make the mistakes of yesterday again. *You have more knowledge today than you have ever had in your whole lifetime.* You have learned from the pain. You have learned from your losses. You have watched carefully and documented what has happened in other people's lives.

Do not fear that yesterday will crawl behind you like a predator and choke you to death.

It will not happen. "Remember ye not the former things, neither consider the things of old. Behold, I will do a new thing; now it shall spring forth; shall ye not know it? I will even make a way in the wilderness, and rivers in the desert," (Isaiah 43:18-19).

"Forgetting those things which are behind, and reaching forth unto those things which are before, I press toward the mark for the prize of the high calling of God in Christ Jesus," (Philippians 3:13-14).

*The Holy Spirit is your Enabler.* "But ye shall receive power, after that the Holy Ghost is come upon you," (Acts 1:8).

*The Holy Spirit is your Comforter.* "But when the Comforter is come, whom I will send unto you from the Father, even the Spirit of truth, which proceedeth from the Father, He shall testify of Me," (John 15:26).

*The Holy Spirit is your Teacher.* "He shall teach you all things, and bring all things to your remembrance, whatsoever I have said unto you," (John 14:26).

*The Holy Spirit is the Revealer of those things which are to come.* "Howbeit when He, the Spirit of truth, is come, He will guide you into all truth," (John 16:13).

It fascinates me that Ruth was willing to leave everything comfortable to pursue her future. Her kinfolks were in her past. She refused to let her upbringing and her religious background become the noose around her neck that sabotaged her future. *She refused to let her past rob her of the potential of tomorrow.*

*Intolerance of The Present Schedules Your Future.* As long as you can *adapt* to the present...you really do not have a future.

Ruth *refused* to build her future around her past. Some of us remember painful experiences from yesterday. We have built our entire lifestyle around that experience. Our conversations are consumed with occurrences of 10 years ago.

This is dangerous.

It is devastating.

When you discuss your past...*you perpetuate it.*

*Words impart life.* When you continually replay painful confrontations and situations of the past, you are giving life to them and a future.

*Leaders permit yesterday to die.*

Ruth did. She did not try to "straddle the fence." She refused to become the link between the past and her future.

She totally abandoned the empty relationships of her past.

One of the saddest pictures is seen in the life of the great patriarch, Abraham. He insisted on bringing

Lot, his nephew, with him into the future God had prepared. Lot was a distraction. Most of Abraham's continual problems could be traced to the *presence of Lot.* You see, God had told him to leave his kinfolks and move to a different territory. He *insisted* on bringing someone he was comfortable with—*to the detriment of his future.*

*Yesterday People Rarely Enjoy Your Future.*

It is natural and normal to want to bring everyone close to us into the chapters of our future success. *Few will qualify.*

Your future must be earned.

It is not guaranteed. It is not the same for everyone. Your future is a Harvest produced by the Seeds you are willing to sow. Bringing yesterday people into the future is like using old wineskins for the new wine of tomorrow. It simply will not work.

*Prepare to enter your future without Yesterday people.* God will bring the right associations with you...or He has scheduled outstanding Divine connections beyond your greatest and wildest dreams.

*Move away from yesterday.* You have exhausted its benefits. Refuse to waste your energy on repairing it. Rather, rebuild by focusing on your future. Certainly, yesterday can be a reservoir of Wisdom and information. You are not forfeiting loyalty. You are not forgetting the precious lives that God used mightily for your continual survival and success. You are, however, refusing to abort your future joys and victories by replaying the memories of yesterday's painful experiences.

Paul refused to wallow in the tears of his past. Few made greater mistakes than he. He caused people to be cast into prison. Christians were murdered because of him. He held the coats of those who stoned Stephen, the great deacon. Yet, he refused to forfeit his future by focusing on his past.

His mistakes were *over.*

His sins were *behind* him.

His name had been changed.

Eventually, you will be forced to make a major decision in your life. *It will be the decision to totally abandon your memories, and empty your energy into the palace of your future.*

Your conversation must become more creative. Start using your imagination instead of your memories. Meet new friends. Experience new places.

*Ruth knew when she had exhausted the benefits of her present season.* This is so powerful and important. Every season in your life contains certain advantages. Whether it is one month of a relationship or 90 days on a job, you must discern the Divine purposes of God in every situation in your life. You must discern the Divine purpose of God in every relationship.

*Never linger in a conversation with someone when it is over.* Would you keep chewing the same mouthful of food for 3 hours? Would you keep reading the same page of a book for 3 days? Would you leave a broken record on at the same groove replaying the same note over and over again for several hours? Would you keep brushing your teeth for 12 hours in a row? Of course you would not.

*When something is finished, it is finished.*

Discern it. Recognize it. Look for it. Consistently be intuitive and discerning when a specific season in your life has concluded. Then, move *quickly* and *expectantly* to the next season God has arranged for you.

This quality makes Achievers unforgettable.

*Make Tomorrow Bigger Than Yesterday.*

This is One of the Secrets to becoming an Uncommon Leader.

RECOMMENDED INVESTMENTS:
Dream Seeds (Book/B-11/106 pages)
Seeds of Wisdom on Dreams & Goals (Book/B-13/32 pages)
Secrets of The Journey, Vol. 7 (Book/B-103/32 pages)
**Order Online Today..! MikeMurdockBooks.com**

# ❧ 8 ❧

# PROTECT YOUR PASSION AT ALL COST

━━━━►❯-◦-❮◄━━━━

*Passion Is Power.*
Pour all of yourself into your leadership role. "And whatsoever ye do, do it heartily, as to the Lord, and not unto men," (Colossians 3:23).

You will never have significant success with anything until it becomes *an Obsession* with you. An Obsession is when something consumes your thoughts and time.

*You will only be remembered for your Obsession.* "For the Son of man is come to seek and to save that which was lost," (Luke 19:10). "God anointed Jesus of Nazareth with the Holy Ghost and with power: Who went about doing good, and healing all that were oppressed of the devil; for God was with Him," (Acts 10:38).

*Uncommon Leaders Fight For One Focus.* Jesus focused on doing the exact instructions of His Heavenly Father. He healed the sick. He noticed the lonely. He came to make people successful, to restore and repair their lives to full fellowship with His Father.

*Your Leadership will cost you...Everything. That Obsession took Jesus to the cross.* It took Him to the crucifixion. Eight inches of thorns were crushed into

His brow. A spear punctured His side. Spikes were driven into His hands. Thirty-nine stripes of a whip tore His back to shreds. Four hundred soldiers spit on His body. His beard was ripped off His face. *He was obsessed with the salvation of mankind...*and He succeeded.

You may start small. You may start with very little. If what you love begins to consume your mind, your thoughts, your conversation, your schedule...look for extraordinary success.

Do you dread going to work every morning? Do you anxiously look at the clock toward closing time each afternoon? Is your mind wandering throughout the day towards other places or things you would love to be doing? Then you will probably not have much success at what you are doing.

Find something that consumes you...something that is worthy of building your entire life around. Empty yourself into it.

*Protect Your Passion At All Cost.*

This is One of the Secrets to becoming an Uncommon Leader.

# ~ 9 ~
# CREATE YOUR DREAM WALL AND UPDATE IT CONTINUOUSLY

*Decide What You Really Want.*

In 1952, a prominent university discovered that only 3 out of 100 graduates had written down a clear list of goals. Ten years later, their follow-up study showed that 3 percent of the graduating class had accomplished more financially than the remaining 97 percent of the class.

Those 3 percent were the *same graduates* who had *written down their goals.*

When you decide exactly *what* you want, the *how to* will emerge.

*Jesus knew His purpose and mission.* "For the Son of man is come to seek and to save that which was lost," (Luke 19:10).

*He knew the product He had to offer.* "The thief cometh not, but for to steal, and to kill, and to destroy: I am come that they might have life, and that they might have it more abundantly," (John 10:10).

*Jesus had a sense of destiny.* He knew where He wanted to go. He knew where people needed Him. (See John 4:3.)

*Jesus knew that leaders were detail-oriented.* "For which of you, intending to build a tower, sitteth not down first, and counteth the cost, whether he have sufficient to finish it?" (Luke 14:28).

Take 4 sheets of paper. At the top of sheet number one, write, "My Lifetime Dreams And Goals."

Now write in total detail everything you would like to become, do or have during your lifetime. *Dream your dreams in detail on paper.*

Now, take sheet number two and write, "My 12 Month Goals."

Now list everything you want to get done within the next 12 months.

Now, take the third sheet of paper and write, "My 30 Day Goals."

Now write out in detail what you would like to accomplish for the next 30 days.

Now, take a fourth sheet of paper and write, "My Ideal Success Daily Routine."

Now write down the 6 most important things you will do in the next 24 hours.

Set your goals.

*Your goals will change throughout your life.*

Someday, you will look back at this very moment and be amazed at your present goals. Things so vital to you at 20 years of age will become unimportant to you at 30.

When I was beginning my ministry, I wanted very much to minister in many different states and cities. Times have changed. Today, staying home excites me. Knowing that my books are being read in many places is far more satisfying to me than traveling. The greatest goal of my life today is staying in my Secret Place of prayer and writing what The Holy Spirit teaches me through His Word and daily experiences.

*These kinds of good changes will happen to you, too.*

## 6 Helpful Tips Concerning Your Dreams And Goals

**1.    Invest One Hour In Writing Down Clearly The Goals That Really Matter To You At This Point.** "Write the vision, and make it plain upon tables, that he may run that readeth it," (Habakkuk 2:2).

**2.    Permit Unexciting Dreams of Yesterday To Die.** Stop pursuing something that does not have the ability to excite you anymore.   Do not feel obligated to keep trying to obtain it...if you are in a different place in your life.

**3.    Do Not Depend On Others To Understand Your Dreams And Goals.**   Permit them their individuality, also.   They have every right to love the things they love.   However, refuse to be intimidated by their efforts to persuade you to move in a different direction with your life.

**4.    Never Make Permanent Decisions Because of Temporary Feelings.**   One young lady got so excited about a new friend that she dropped the lease on her own apartment to move in with her friend.   Within a week, she realized her mistake!

**5.    Avoid Intimate Relationships With Those Who Do Not Really Respect Your Dreams.** You will have to sever ties.   *Wrong people do not always leave your life voluntarily.*   Life is too short to permit discouragers close to you.   "And have no fellowship with the unfruitful works of darkness, but rather reprove them," (Ephesians 5:11).

**6.    Anticipate Changes In Your Goals.**   Your present feelings and opinions are not permanent.

New experiences are coming. New relationships are ahead. Stay conscious of this.

When you assess and evaluate your goals, you will unclutter your life of the unnecessary.

*Create Your Dream Wall And Update It Continuously.*

This is One of the Secrets to becoming an Uncommon Leader.

# ❧ 10 ❧
# FIGHT TO KEEP THE SPIRIT OF A FINISHER

*Leaders Are Finishers.*

Completion creates pleasure. "The desire accomplished is sweet to the soul," (Proverbs 13:19).

It is fun to be creative. It is exciting to always give birth to new ideas, think of new places to go or launch a new product. Real leaders though, complete things. They are *"follow through"* people.

Jesus was 30 years old when He started His ministry. His ministry went for three-and-a-half years. He did many miracles. He touched many lives. He electrified the world through 12 men.

Hidden in the thousands of Scriptures is a Golden Principle that revealed His power. It happened on the horrible day of His crucifixion. He was taunted by thousands. A spear pierced His side. Spikes were driven into His hands. Eight inches of thorns were crushed into His brow. Blood had dried on His hair. Four hundred soldiers left spittle running down his body.

That is when He uttered perhaps the greatest sentence ever uttered on earth: "It is finished," (John 19:30). The sin of man could be forgiven. He paid the price. *The Plan had been completed.* He was the Lamb led to the slaughter.

He was the Chief Cornerstone. "And are built upon the foundation of the apostles and prophets,

Jesus Christ Himself being the chief corner stone," (Ephesians 2:20).

*The Prince of Peace had come.* "For unto us a child is born, unto us a son is given: and the government shall be upon His shoulder: and His name shall be called Wonderful, Counsellor, The mighty God, The everlasting Father, The Prince of Peace," (Isaiah 9:6). Our great High Priest, the Son of God, was our Golden Link to the God of Heaven. (See Hebrews 4:14.)

## *Uncommon Men Are Finishers*

*Jesus was a finisher.* He finished what He started. The bridge that linked man to God was complete. Man could approach God without fear.

*The Apostle Paul was a finisher.* "I have fought a good fight, I have finished my course, I have kept the faith," (2 Timothy 4:7).

*Solomon, the wisest man that ever lived, was a finisher.* "So Solomon built the house, and finished it," (1 Kings 6:14).

One famous multi-millionaire said, "I will pay a great salary to anyone who can complete an instruction that I give him."

Start completing *little things.* Write that "thank you" note to your friend. Make those two telephone calls.

*Embrace the spirit of a finisher.* "And ye shall be hated of all men for My name's sake: but he that endureth to the end shall be saved," (Matthew 10:22).

*Fight To Keep The Spirit of A Finisher.*

This is One of the Secrets to becoming an Uncommon Leader.

# ❧ 11 ❧

# VIEW TIME AS YOUR SEED FOR CHANGE

*Do Not Be Too Hard On Yourself.*

Little-by-little and day-by-day, you will start tasting the rewards of change.

Look at the patience of God with Israel. He "knew they were but flesh." He took many years to even train their leader, Moses. You are not an exception.

*Every man fails.* Leaders simply get back up... and begin again.

## *God Never Hurries*

*Give God time to work.*

Sometimes those things you desire the most may take longer to achieve. It takes longer to make a Rolls Royce automobile than a bicycle.

Millions of miracles have been dashed on the "rocks of impatience." Give God time.

Something good is happening that you do not see. Wait joyfully with great expectation.

"The Lord upholdeth all that fall, and raiseth up all those that be bowed down," (Psalm 145:14).

"And let us not be weary in well doing: for in due season we shall reap, if we faint not," (Galatians 6:9).

## *Unwrap The Gift of Today Slowly, Carefully And With Great Expectation*

Your *Present* contains Secrets.

Your *Present* contains Gold.

Your *Present* contains Hidden Wisdom.

Your *Present* is a Divine Link.

Your *Present* is a Wealth of Wisdom.

*Your Present Season Contains Benefits That Your Hurrying Will Abort.*

Have you *exhausted* the scrutiny of your *Present* season, benefits and relationships? Few have. Few do.

There is an exceptional Scripture that poured out of the heart of the psalmist. "Wait on the Lord: be of good courage, and He shall strengthen thine heart: wait, I say, on the Lord," (Psalm 27:14). Examine the guaranteed Harvest of patience and tenacious focus on the Secret of Waiting. "He shall strengthen thine heart."

*Strength* is the promise here.

*Strength* is the golden Harvest.

*Strength* is the promised dividend from the investment of...waiting.

*Strength is promised throughout Scripture for those who become entwined with God.* "But they that wait upon the Lord shall renew their strength; they shall mount up with wings as eagles; they shall run, and not be weary; and they shall walk, and not faint," (Isaiah 40:31).

*View Time As Your Seed For Change.*

This is One of the Secrets to becoming an Uncommon Leader.

# ≈ 12 ≈

# IDENTIFY TIME-WASTERS AND CREATE THE SYSTEM THAT PROTECTS YOU FROM THEM

*Your Daily Agenda...Is Your Life.*

You cannot save time. You cannot *collect* time. You cannot place it in a special bank vault. You are only permitted to *spend* it...wisely or foolishly. You must do *something* with time.

You will invest it or you will waste it.

Everyone has a hidden agenda. Those around you will be reaching to pull you "off course." You must be careful to protect your list of priorities.

## *Jesus Valued His Chosen Schedule Above The Requests of Friends*

Jesus did. There is a fascinating story in the Bible about it.

Lazarus, a close friend of Jesus, became sick. Mary and Martha, his two sisters, sent word to Jesus to come. "When He had heard therefore that he was sick, He abode two days still in the same place where He was," (John 11:6). Mary was upset, "Then said Martha unto Jesus, Lord, if Thou hadst been here, my brother had not died," (John 11:21).

Jesus had deliberately delayed His coming. *He*

*kept His own schedule.* He protected His agenda. He did not allow the emergencies of others to get Him off track. *He guarded His list of priorities.*

## Train Gatekeepers To Handle Your Phone Calls And Email

Only you know your priorities.

*Make today count.* Remember the 24 golden box cars on the track of success. If you do not control what goes into each of your 24 golden box cars (hours)...somebody else will.

Avoid distractions. Write your daily list of things to do. Protect your schedule. *This is your life.* Make it happen.

Provide your Secretary or Personal Assistant the List of Access Circles for those who phone. Example:

Circle A: You will accept phone calls *at any time.*

Circle B: You will return phone calls within 2 hours.

Circle C: Someone else should return the call for you.

*Identify Time-Wasters And Create The System That Protects You From Them.*

This is One of the Secrets to becoming an Uncommon Leader.

# ❧ **13** ❧

# ASK QUALITY QUESTIONS

*Ask Questions.*

Listening is a Divine command. "Hear counsel, and receive instruction, that thou mayest be wise in thy latter end," (Proverbs 19:20).

Ask questions to accurately determine the needs and desires of others.

Interrogate your world. Insist on listening to the opinions and needs of others.

Almost nobody on earth listens to others, nor questions them.

It is a Master Secret of Success.

Our Master Mentor was genius in questioning.

*Jesus asked questions.*

Once when Simon Peter went fishing, he caught nothing. When the morning was come, Jesus was standing on the shore. Jesus calls out, "Then Jesus saith unto them, Children, have ye any meat? They answered Him, No," (John 21:5). *He assumed nothing. He pursued information.*

His *question* was His entry point into their life. He had something they needed. He had information.

His question was a link to their future...the Bridge for their relationship. He then instructed them, "Cast the net on the right side of the ship, and ye shall find," (John 21:6).

Information is the difference between your

Present and your Future.

## *8 Facts About Questions*

1.   **Asking Questions Is A Command.**
2.   **Asking Questions Reveals The Needs of Others.**
3.   **Asking Questions Creates An Entry Point Into Another Life.**
4.   **Asking Questions Reveals Passion.**
5.   **Asking Questions Reveals Caring.**
6.   **Asking Questions Removes Doubt.**
7.   **Asking Questions Dissolves Fears.**
8.   **Asking Questions Is A Seed For Change.**

## *Create Your Information System*

Document the needs of others. Keep a rolodex. Maintain your information in your personal computer or a notebook of their needs and desires. What are your Team Managers' needs today? Are you really listening to them? Do they really feel you are listening to them? Most employees feel that their bosses really do not hear their complaints. Most employers feel that their employees do not interpret them correctly.

*Jesus pursued information.*
*Ask Quality Questions...continually.*
This is One of the Secrets to becoming an Uncommon Leader.

# ≈ 14 ≈

# TRAIN YOUR MANAGERS TO BECOME MASTER PROBLEM-SOLVERS

———————————————

*You Are Here For A Reason.*

To assign means to set apart or mark for a specific purpose. "But know that the Lord hath set apart him that is godly for Himself," (Psalm 4:3).

The Bible, the "Manufacturer's Handbook," is filled with examples of those who discovered and embraced their Assignment.

▶ *Moses* solved problems for the *Israelites.*

▶ *Aaron* solved problems for *Moses.*

▶ *Jonathan* was assigned to *David.*

▶ *Jonah* was assigned to the *Ninevites.*

▶ A *handmaiden* helped *Naaman* get healed.

▶ *Ruth* was assigned to *Naomi.*

You too, are assigned to solve problems...for somebody...somewhere.

You are the *Healer* for someone sick.

You are the *Life Jacket* for someone drowning.

You are the *Ruler* over someone unruly.

You are the *Lifter* for someone fallen.

You have asked these questions a thousand times. Why am I here? Why *me?* What is my *purpose?*

Is there *really* a God? Where did I come from? Did I exist in another world before this one?

A poem is the proof of a *poet*.

A song is the proof of the *composer*.

A product is the proof of a *manufacturer*.

Creation is the proof of the *Creator*.

*Why were you born?* It is an excellent question. It is a wonderful question. It is a frequent question. It is an *answerable* question. You deserve an answer. The answer exists. The answers are clear. The answers are more obvious than many realize.

The *Manufacturer* is God.

The *Product* is You.

The *Manual* is the Bible.

*You were created to bring pleasure to God.* "For thou hast created all things, and for thy pleasure they are and were created," (Revelation 4:11).

*You have been set apart for an exclusive purpose and reason.* "But know that the Lord hath set apart him that is godly for himself," (Psalm 4:3).

*You will give an account of your conduct and productivity.* "So then every one of us shall give account of himself to God," (Romans 14:12).

Every product contains more answers than we first realized. *Study the car.* The fact that it *moves* is proof that it has a different *purpose* than your home. Compare a baseball bat and a sandwich. The hardness of one and the softness of the other is an obvious clue that their purpose *differs*.

*Studying your difference rather than your similarity to others will produce an incredible revelation of Wisdom...*especially regarding your Assignment—the problem you were created to solve.

Mechanics solve *car* problems.

Lawyers solve *legal* problems.

Ministers solve *spiritual* problems.

I had an interesting experience during a recent telephone conversation. While talking to someone very important in my life, I realized suddenly that I was merely *listening.* In fact, they asked me nothing. He did not ask me for my opinion, or feelings or observations. I waited patiently. Then, I thought, "Why am I even listening to this when he obviously does not want solutions? If he wanted solutions, he would be asking me questions." Then it dawned on me. My *listening* was his solution. He simply needed someone to listen to his pain, discomfort and heartache. Yes, even listening to someone hurting near you is often a marvelous therapy and solution to their problem.

Motivational speakers receive thousands of dollars to solve a problem for salesmen in a company. Effective counselors make an excellent living simply by being willing to listen patiently, thoughtfully and consistently to their clients.

Sometimes *words* heal.

Sometimes *silence* heals.

Sometimes *listening* heals.

It is important that you *recognize* your Assignment. It is essential that you embrace the *difference* in your Assignment. It is important that you are *willing to be mentored* for your Assignment.

Your function is *different* from others.

The function of others is different from yours.

Counselors provide *answers* to problems.

Comedians provide *escape* from problems.

## *Your Priority As A Leader*

Now, think about your managers or others under your supervision. Your focus must become... Mentoring them in solving their own problems.

## *9 Facts Your Managers Should Be Taught*

1. *Problems Are The Gates To Your Significance.*
2. *Problems Are Wonderful, Glorious Seeds For Change.*
3. *Problems Link You To Others.*
4. *Problems Provide Your Income.*
5. *Problems Birth Opportunity To Reveal Your Uniqueness.*
6. *Problems Birth New Relationships.*
7. *Problems Are The Real Reason Friendships Exist.*
8. *Remove Problems From The Earth, And You Will Destroy Any Sense of Significance In Humanity.*
9. *Problems Bring Good People Together During Bad Times.*

The mechanic knows that an automobile problem is his *connection* to you.

The dentist knows that a tooth problem is his *connection* to you.

The problem God created you to solve on earth is called your Assignment.

*Train Your Managers To Become Master Problem-Solvers.*

This is One of the Secrets to becoming an Uncommon Leader.

# ∞ 15 ∞

# ANTICIPATE AND AVOID UNNECESSARY CONFLICT

*Many Battles Produce Little Reward.*
Identify quickly those who are difficult to please. Be honest.

## *Why Contentious People Are Deadly*

**1. Conflict Distracts You From Your Dreams And Goals.** By the way, a contentious person often considers themselves very honest and up front. In fact, they usually take pride in telling you "the way things really are." Subconsciously, they are often modeling someone in their life (a father or mother) who accomplished their goals through *intimidation.* Subconsciously, they admire this person and have decided to follow that pattern, failing to see the losses created through this kind of attitude.

**2. Nothing Is More Harmful To A Company Than A Contentious Employee.** Every boss knows this. When an employee cannot get along with other employees, profits are lost. That employee becomes costly. *Focus is broken.* Other employees become emotionally fragmented. Important projects are delayed.

**3. Contentious People Destroy The Momentum, Bonding And Synergy That Agreement Can Create.** "Mark them which cause divisions and offenses contrary to the doctrine which ye have learned; and avoid them," (Romans 16:17).

**4.     A Contentious Person Is Always A Door For Satan To Launch Every Evil Work In An Organization.**     "For where envying and strife is, there is confusion and every evil work," (James 3:16).

**5.     Contentious People Often Sabotage The Work of God.**     Many years ago I heard one of the most startling statements from a famous missionary. I was sitting under some huge trees in East Africa. Monkeys were jumping from tree limb to tree limb. My precious missionary friend explained the number one reason some missionaries never fulfill their full term on the field. (I thought missionaries came home due to sickness, culture shock or lack of finances.)

"Mike, the number one reason missionaries do not stay on the mission field is their inability to get along with other missionaries."   Think about it. Missionaries, who should be obsessed with sharing the Gospel, often return home because of their failure to create harmony and an environment of agreement.

**6.     Contention Is Contagious.**     When someone permits the spirit of conflict and disputing to enter their life, they will influence and affect *everyone* around them. I have seen a happy, peaceful household turn argumentative within 30 minutes when a contentious person entered the room. That person carried the spirit of contention with them.

**7.     You Can Succeed Almost Anywhere Else, Except With A Contentious Person.**     "It is better to dwell in the corner of the housetop, than with a brawling woman and in a wide house," (Proverbs 25:24).

## *Who Are Your Trouble-Makers?*

**Conflict Always Begins With A Person...Not**

Merely An Issue.

**1.    Contentious People Are In Total Opposition To The Law of Agreement, The Greatest Law of Success On Earth.** "Two are better than one; because they have a good reward for their labour.  For if they fall, the one will lift up his fellow:  but woe to him that is alone when he falleth; for he hath not another to help him up," (Ecclesiastes 4:9-10).

**2.    Contentious People Discuss Situations That Do Not Involve Themselves.**  This is one evidence of a contentious person.  They discuss the business of *others*.  "He that passeth by, and meddleth with strife belonging not to him, is like one that taketh a dog by the ears," (Proverbs 26:17).

**3.    A Contentious Person Enjoys Debate, Disputings And Opposing Whatever Has Been Spoken.**  A contentious person always looks for a reason to disagree about something.  They ignore every point of agreement.

**4.    A Contentious Person Is In Opposition To Godly Wisdom.**  "But the Wisdom that is from above is first pure, then peaceable, gentle, and easy to be intreated, full of mercy and good fruits, without partiality, and without hypocrisy," (James 3:17).

**5.    A Contentious Attitude And Spirit Is Always Birthed By Unthankfulness.**  It is a sin that God abhors.  It was the first sin ever committed.  Satan was unthankful for his position and chose to fight for a change.  *Ingratitude is poisonous.*  It can destroy a family within weeks.  It can ruin a successful organization within months.  Churches exploding with growth have fragmented within weeks when a spirit of ingratitude infected the congregation.

## *How To Respond To Contentious People*

**1.    The Character of A Contentious Person Is Only Revealed When You Rebuke Them.**  If he is a scorner and fool, he will hate you.  If he is a wise person simply needing correction, he will love you. "Reprove not a scorner, lest he hate thee:  rebuke a wise man, and he will love thee," (Proverbs 9:8).

**2.    Any Contentious Conversation Must Be Boldly Faced And Stopped Immediately.** Interrupt the conversation with, "It is wonderful how God will turn this for our good!  I am so thankful for what He is about to do!  We have a wonderful God!"  It will be like throwing cold water on a destructive fire.

**3.    The Contentious Person Must Be Confronted Honestly And Courageously About Their Attitude.**  Others are bold enough to poison your climate and atmosphere with "arrows of unthankfulness" piercing the air.  So, dominate your turf.  Take charge.  Use your words to turn the tide.

**4.    Any Contentious Person Who Refuses To Change Must Not Continue To Have Access To You.**  "Where no wood is, there the fire goeth out: so where there is no talebearer, the strife ceaseth.  As coals are to burning coals, and wood to fire; so is a contentious man to kindle strife," (Proverbs 26:20-21). Your attitude is a *personal decision.*  Your attitude is a *mood* created by your chosen focus.

Agreement is the greatest enemy satan has ever faced.

*Anticipate And Avoid Unnecessary Conflict.*

This is One of the Secrets to becoming an Uncommon Leader.

# ≈ 16 ≈

# INVEST THE TIME NECESSARY TO NEGOTIATE EFFECTIVELY

*Negotiate Everything.*

I walked into a luggage store in Dallas many years ago. When I had selected the luggage I desired, I asked the young lady if she could provide a "corporate discount."

"What is a corporate discount?"

"Forty percent off."

"All right!" was her reply.

With one simple question, I saved several hundred dollars. *Negotiate everything.*

While standing at the airline counter, I was informed that my excess baggage was over $200.

"I was hoping you would show me a little mercy today," I joked gently.

The agent thought for a few moments and replied, "All right." With one simple statement, I saved over $200.

*Negotiate everything.* Your *words* are creating financial gain or loss.

Your *words* are bringing increase or decrease.

Your *words* are creating doors or walls.

Your *words* are bridges or barricades.

The Scripture teaches it: "A man shall eat good by the fruit of his mouth: but the soul of the transgressors shall eat violence," (Proverbs 13:2). "The wicked is snared by the transgression of his lips: but the just shall come out of trouble," (Proverbs 12:13).

## *8 Facts Every Leader Should Remember In Negotiating Effectively*

**Pursue Negotiation Wisdom.**

**1. Attend Negotiation Seminars, Listen To Tapes And Secure The Counsel of Qualified Mentors Before Doing Any Serious Negotiation.**

**2. Successful Negotiation Requires The Right Attitude.** Nobody wants to be taken lightly, intimidated or pushed. Everybody is involved. The lady in the luggage store wanted to sell the luggage, create favor and a happy customer. I gave her the information which would accommodate that need, a 40 percent discount. (I later returned to buy many other items because of the favor she showed.)

The airline that graciously permitted me the excess baggage has become my favorite airline receiving over $100,000 of my business each year.

Negotiation must be viewed as a win-win situation for everybody involved.

**3. Successful Negotiation Requires An Understanding of The Cost Involved For Others.** Donald Trump explained why his father was so successful in negotiating prices. His father invested time in finding out the exact cost for those with whom he was negotiating. This enabled him to know exactly how far to negotiate.

**4. Successful Negotiation Requires Proper Timing.** Many years ago I was very weary when I arrived home from a meeting. The flight was tiresome. As I walked into the office, a staff member approached me.

"I have got to talk to you!"

"All right. Sit down. How can I help you?"

She was very aggressive and flippant. "I need a raise!"

"Well, how much are you wanting me to increase your salary each month?" I asked.

"I need a $1,000 a month raise."

I almost laughed. I really thought she was joking. She was not. She continued, "My husband and I are moving into a new home that we have just built, and I really need the income to pay for the house."

It was ridiculous to me, I almost laughed aloud. I proceeded to advise her *gently* that, perhaps, it would be well for her to find another job where she could secure the salary she needed. I asked, "Your present salary was created by a list of problems you chose to solve for me. Now you want a huge increase in salary. Do you have a list of the new problems you will begin to solve for me?"

It had never crossed her mind to solve more problems for her new salary.

**5.    Successful Negotiation Involves Long-Term Gain, Not Short-Term Gain.** The famous billionaire, Sam Walton, said he never invested in a company for where it would be in 18 months. He invested in companies that would succeed 10 years down the road. An employee can often squeeze out an extra dollar from a boss during a crisis situation. If it creates a wall of separation though, that staff person can cause a deeper problem in the long-term.

**6.    Successful    Negotiation    Requires Quality Time.** Do not rush anything. You will never do well in something that has not taken thought... sufficient time to collect information and necessary data. Run from the salesman who insists that "this is the last day of this sale." Do not fall for it. When you return a month later, they will still deal! They need your purchase more than they need their own product.

**7. Listen Longer To The Needs of Others.** Listeners are rare. You are developing an understanding of the concerns, fears and passion of the hearts of those at the negotiating table. Wisdom is worth any price. *Invest the time* to listen thoroughly, compassionately and expectantly.

**8. Successful Negotiation Should Focus On Details That Matter The Most.** Several years ago, an impressive young couple wrote me about a job. He was making $5 an hour. He was riding a motorcycle to his second job. He had two jobs at $10 an hour total. They were destitute. My heart went out to them. They had driven all night to meet me face-to-face for an interview. I agreed to pay him for 8 hours a day what both his jobs were presently providing for working 16 hours a day. Then, as a gesture of caring, I included their housing if they would do additional yard work at my home. They were thrilled and elated. Over a period of time, I purchased furniture, dishes, clothes and so forth. They were enjoyable, so I was happy to do so.

Soon, someone must have inspired them to negotiate for more. At every opportunity to "squeeze me," such as appliance breakdowns...they pushed. I noticed a pattern. It became one-sided.

When you have many employees, you cannot give everybody a raise when you desire. You can not always give it to them the moment they deserve it. *You have to think long-term for the organization.* Something within me became agitated. When the oven broke down, they wanted me to replace it. I was weary of replacing everything. I requested that they pay half, and I would pay the other half. They attempted to use harsh words to negotiate with me. I am not the kind of person who responds well to intimidation.

I realized they were frustrated, so I explained that they had 45 days to go find a new house, and they could purchase it themselves. Yes, they were good people, but were poor at negotiation. They lost a wonderful blessing trying to squeeze "an extra nickel." Do not lose dollars trying to save pennies.

Yes, I agree, your opinion deserves to be heard.

However, make certain that it is heard at the *right time* in the *right environment* and with the *right attitude.*

Negotiate everything.

*Invest The Time Necessary To Negotiate Effectively.*

This is One of the Secrets to becoming an Uncommon Leader.

What You Are Is Revealed
By What You Do;
What You Do Reveals
What You Really Believe.

-MIKE MURDOCK

# ❧ 17 ❧

# SEIZE EVERY OPPORTUNITY TO ESTABLISH YOUR INTEGRITY

*People Talk.*

The Biblical account of Ruth includes the reputation she built.

Boaz describes it this way, "And Boaz answered and said unto her, *It hath fully been shewed me,* all that thou hast done unto thy mother in law since the death of thine husband: and how thou hast left thy father and thy mother, and the land of thy nativity, and art come unto a people which thou knewest not heretofore," (Ruth 2:11).

***A Good Reputation Is The Master Secret For Uncommon Blessing.***

Later he spoke, "Blessed be thou of the Lord, my daughter: for thou hast shewed more kindness in the latter end than at the beginning, inasmuch as thou followedst not young men, whether poor or rich. And now, my daughter, fear not; I will do to thee all that thou requirest: *for all the city of my people doth know that thou art a virtuous woman,*" (Ruth 3:10-11).

*People talk...*good things and bad things. False accusations and current assessments.

*People spoke well of Ruth.* Her sacrificial attitude and dedication to preserving and maintaining the life of her widowed mother-in-law was a known fact in the community. Obviously, she had not even dated or bonded with any of the young men in the city—poor or rich. Her total focus was on Naomi.

***Your Productivity Affects Your Reputation.***
This had registered heavily in the heart and mind of Boaz who did not hesitate to respond to her pursuit of him.

***Others Should Commend You.*** "Let another man praise thee, and not thine own mouth; a stranger, and not thine own lips," (Proverbs 27:2).

***Reputation Is More Powerful Than Money.***
"A good name is rather to be chosen than great riches, and loving favour rather than silver and gold," (Proverbs 22:1).

***A Good Name Is More Magnetic Than A Strong Fragrance.*** "A good name is better than precious ointment; and the day of death than the day of one's birth," (Ecclesiastes 7:1).

## *Listen For Deception*

Several years ago, I arrived at the house of a young lady to take her to supper. As we were driving to the restaurant she remarked, "I had another date planned tonight, but I told him I had to visit a relative in the hospital."

She had *lied*. It sickened me. I had been excited about establishing a relationship with her only to find out within minutes that falsehood came naturally and easily to her. Obviously, I would be the next victim on her list. It was the first and last date I had with her.

Whatever it takes...*develop integrity*.

Focus on it. Carefully examine each word and

sentence that comes from your lips. Never say anything insincere. Refuse to brag on someone's singing if it is untrue. Do not say things merely to encourage others. "Recompense to no man evil for evil. Provide things honest in the sight of all men," (Romans 12:17).

The *compassion* of Ruth was known.

Observe how a woman speaks to her mother. Note well how a man treats his mother. Also, observe how he reacts to the struggle and heartaches of the unfortunate.

Ruth's purity and virtue were known.

The entire town knew of her obsession and kindness to her mother-in-law. They said she treated her mother-in-law better than 7 sons would treat a mother. That kind of treatment is almost unheard of today.

This does not mean you have to advertise all your good deeds. It is not important that you trumpet to the world all your acts of kindness and mercy. Somehow, God has a way of "letting your integrity be made known."

## *Stay Clean During Seasons of False Accusation*

Admittedly, many false accusations are hurled these days. Good people have been stained through vindictive and violent people. Joseph is not the only story where someone who walked in total integrity before the Lord had his reputation devastated by those who were refused or ignored.

*What you are...will eventually be exposed and*

*known.* Yes, integrity and loyalty are marvelous qualities that make you unforgettable.

*Seize Every Opportunity To Establish Your Integrity.*

This is One of the Secrets to becoming an Uncommon Leader.

RECOMMENDED INVESTMENTS:
Dream Seeds (Book/B-11/106 pages)
Seeds of Wisdom on Dreams & Goals (Book/B-13/32 pages)
Secrets of The Journey, Vol. 6 (Book/B-102/32 pages)
**Order Online Today..! MikeMurdockBooks.com**

# ≈ 18 ≈

# MASTER THE ART OF EXIT

*Relationships Do Not Always Last Forever.*

But, it is important to exit every door of friendship *appropriately*. You cannot enter the next season of your life with joy unless you exit your present season correctly.

## *Uncommon Leaders Have Mastered The Art of Exit*

Jesus *finished* His work on earth. He cried out from the cross, "It is finished!" Salvation was complete. Redemption had taken place. He had paid the price for the sins of man. Three days later, the resurrection would take place. He would return to the Father where He would make intercession for you and me. He finished *properly*—with the approval of the Father.

Solomon *finished* the temple. It was an incredible feat. Some value his temple today at over $500 billion dollars. He was respected, pursued and celebrated. He completed what he started.

Paul *finished* his course. He fought a good fight, kept the faith, and finished his course. (Read 2 Timothy 4:7.) He was a success in the eyes of God. He made his exit from his earthly ministry with grace, passion and dignity.

Your life is a collection of *beginnings*.

It is also a collection of *exits*.

You will not stay in your present job forever. You will someday leave your present position. Your supervisor today could be another acquaintance in your life next year. Close the relationship with dignity.

## 8 Keys To Remember When A Relationship Is Ending

Are you leaving your organization? Are you terminating an incompetent, disloyal or unhappy employee? These are helpful reminders every Leader should remember.

**1. Close Every Door Gently.** Do not slam Doors. Do not kick Doors. Do not yell at Doors. *They are Doors through which you may need to return again in the future.* The attitude of your exit determines if you can ever walk back through that door again. "A soft answer turneth away wrath: but grievous words stir up anger," (Proverbs 15:1).

**2. Close Doors With Forgiveness.** Unforgiveness is poisonous. It is the cancer that will destroy you from within. Release others to God. Permit Him to do the penalizing or correcting. Like Joseph, recognize that the ultimate plan of God will bring your promotion. (See Romans 8:28.)

**3. Close Doors With Kindness.** If your fianceé leaves you with cutting and bitter words, thank The Holy Spirit for salvaging you. Perhaps she was not your *Proverbs 31 Woman* after all for "in her tongue is the law of kindness," (Proverbs 31:26).

**4. Close Every Door With Promises Fulfilled.** Do not leave your job until you have finished what you promised. Complete every vow... *whatever* the cost. Integrity is easy to test. Simply ask, "Did I fulfill my promise?" (See Ecclesiastes 5:4-5.)

When people lose you in the "forest of words," apply the Principle of Vow Fulfillment. Forget the blaming, complaining and accusations. This principle reveals everything you need to know about another.

**5. Close Every Door With Integrity.** Few will do it. People are rarely angry for the reason they tell you. Much is never discussed. The trap of deception is deadly. It begins when you deceive yourself...then those around you. Always be honest to others about the *reason* for the doors closing. It is not necessary to give every detail. It is important that the details you give are *accurate.*

**6. Close Every Door With Courage.** It is not always easy to close a door that The Holy Spirit requires you to close. Closing *that* door requires Uncommon Courage to face the future without that person. Remember The precious Holy Spirit will never leave you nor forsake you. (See John 14:16.) He opens doors. He closes doors. He is the Bridge to every person in your future.

**7. Close Every Door With Expectation of Promotion.** "For promotion cometh neither from the east, nor from the west, nor from the south. But God is the judge: He putteth down one, and setteth up another," (Psalm 75:6-7).

**8. Close Every Door By The Timing of The Holy Spirit.** Do not close it in a fit of anger. Do not close the door because of a misunderstanding that erupts. Do not close it just because someone recommends that you exit. *Know the timing of God.* (Read Ecclesiastes 3:1-8.)

A young man sat in my kitchen a few weeks ago. I was quite concerned. He wanted a position in my ministry. I asked him about his relationship with his previous boss, my preacher friend. He avoided the issue continually. In fact, I had to ask him the question 4 or 5 times before I got a partial answer. At the end of the conversation, he explained his financial dilemma. He had left a job before securing another one. I explained to him how foolish this was. If God were moving him, He would tell him the place he was to go.

When God told Elijah to leave the brook, Zarephath was scheduled. (Read 1 Kings 17.)

When the Israelites left Egypt, Canaan was their determined destination. (Read Exodus 13.)

*God always brings you out of a place to bring you into another place.* Close every door with God's timing. When you close doors gently, news will travel...*good news.*

*Master The Art of Exit.*

This is One of the Secrets to becoming an Uncommon Leader.

# ❧ 19 ❧

# BECOME AN ENEMY TO YOUR WEAKNESS

*Never Trivialize A Weakness In Your Life.*

I have been in the ministry for over 40 years and watched incredible, powerful and extraordinary men fall from their thrones into ashes...good men... articulate men...brilliant men. A *tiny Weakness,* like a small cancer, began to eat its way into their lives. Greed, lust, lying, prayerlessness, gossip grew until that Weakness became a raging inferno. The small puppy became a rabid monster.

Your Weakness may presently be at the embryonic state...perhaps the size of an acorn. Nobody else can see it yet. You may even joke about it, but you cannot afford to play with a Weakness in your life.

You see, when you are not victorious, you will become miserable. That misery creates agitation. Agitation will cause you to lash out at those you love, destroying the very foundation of your life.

## *Your Weakness Will Create Wrong Relationships*

**1.    Somebody Is Assigned By Hell To Fuel And Strengthen Your Weakness.** Delilah was sent by satan to destroy Samson. "And the lords of the Philistines came up unto her, and said unto her, Entice him, and see wherein his great strength lieth, and by what means we may prevail against him, that we may bind him to afflict him: and we will give thee every one of us eleven hundred pieces of silver," (Judges 16:5).

2. **Your Weakness Will Bond You With The Wrong People.** Remember Samson and Delilah? (See Judges 16:4-20.)

3. **Your Weakness Will Embrace And Seize Any Friendship That Permits It, Allows It To Exist And Finds It Tolerable.**

## *Conquering Your Weakness Brings Many Rewards*

1. **Your Victory Over Your Weakness Will Unlock Victories For Others.** This is true, even if they are unaware of your Weakness.

2. **Overcoming Your Weakness Brings Incredible Rewards For All Eternity.** (See Revelation 3.)

3. **The Lives And Futures of Those You Love Are Awaiting Your Overcoming And Triumph Over Your Weakness.** Your victory means victory for them! When David killed Goliath, the entire nation of Israel changed seasons. Your family is sitting in fear of their own Weaknesses that can destroy them. They will be strengthened when they see you victorious over your Weakness.

"He that overcometh shall inherit all things; and I will be his God, and he shall be My son," (Revelation 21:7).

## *What To Do With Your Weakness*

**1. Your Weakness Should Be Confronted When It First Emerges At Its Early Sign of Exposure.**

**2. Few Will Confront Their Weakness With The Proper Weaponry...The Word of God.** "Wherewithal shall a young man cleanse his way? by taking heed thereto according to Thy word," (Psalm 119:9).

**3. Your Weakness Does Not Necessarily Have To Be Confessed To Everybody.** You must admit it to yourself and to your Heavenly Father. "The Lord is nigh unto them that are of a broken heart; and saveth such as be of a contrite spirit," (Psalm 34:18).

**4. Your Heavenly Father Is Fully Aware of Your Weakness.** It matters to Him. He reaches out to you to annihilate it. "For He remembered that they were but flesh; a wind that passeth away, and cometh not again," (Psalm 78:39). "Like as a father pitieth his children, so the Lord pitieth them that fear Him," (Psalm 103:13).

**5. You Must Starve Your Weakness A Day At A Time.** Make no room for the flesh. "But put ye on the Lord Jesus Christ, and make not provision for the flesh, to fulfil the lusts thereof," (Romans 13:14).

**6. When You Justify Your Weakness, It Laughs With Glee Knowing That In Due Time It Will Displace A Strength In Your Life.** Weakness thrives in the climate of acceptance and permission. *Anything Permitted Increases.*

**7. Your Weakness Can Only Be Overcome By The Word of God In Your Life When You Confront It.** Satan attempts to camouflage your

Weakness, wrapping it in acceptable vocabulary. Jesus used The Word as a weapon. (Read Matthew 4:1-11.)

**8. God Makes Every Effort To Reveal Your Weakness To You Before It Destroys You.** "And the Lord said, Simon, Simon, behold, satan hath desired to have you, that he may sift you as wheat," (Luke 22:31).

**9. It Is Possible To Know And Recognize Your Own Weakness Before Others Know It.** Peter discovered this. "Peter answered and said unto Him, Though all men shall be offended because of Thee, yet will I never be offended. Jesus said unto him, Verily I say unto thee, That this night, before the cock crow, thou shalt deny Me thrice. Peter said unto Him, Though I should die with Thee, yet will I not deny Thee. And after a while came unto him they that stood by, and said to Peter, Surely thou also art one of them; for thy speech bewrayeth thee. Then began he to curse and to swear, saying, I know not the man. And immediately the cock crew. And Peter remembered the word of Jesus, which said unto him, Before the cock crow, thou shalt deny Me thrice. And he went out, and wept bitterly," (Matthew 26:33-35, 73-75).

## *Your Weakness Is Conquerable*

**1. Your Weakness Cannot Be Overcome With Humanism, Human Philosophy, Explanations And Self Will-Power.** If your Weakness could be overcome by yourself, the blood of Jesus is powerless and The Holy Spirit is unnecessary. "But ye shall receive power, after that the Holy Ghost is come upon you," (Acts 1:8).

**2. God Will Permit You To Enjoy Many Victories.** Victories can occur when your Weakness is in its *beginning* stages. He is long-suffering and merciful. He gives you chance after chance, opportunity after opportunity to repent and reach for deliverance. Jesus cried, "How often would I have gathered thy children together, even as a hen gathereth her chickens under her wings, and ye would not!" (Matthew 23:37).

**3. God Wants To Grow Your Strength And Destroy Your Weakness.** "Likewise reckon ye also yourselves to be dead indeed unto sin, but alive unto God through Jesus Christ our Lord," (Romans 6:11).

## *Your Weakness Must Be Confronted*

**1. Satan Will Invest Whatever Time Is Necessary To Nurture A Small Weakness Into A Raging Wolf That Destroys You.** Keep resisting. (See Matthew 4:3-10.)

**2. Your Weakness Can Multiply.** A little leaven always leaveneth the whole lump. (Read 1 Corinthians 5:6-8.)

**3. Your Weakness Does Not Want To Stay Small.** It resents being neglected. It envies your gift that continuously increases.

**4. Your Weakness Does Not Want To Remain Insignificant.** It craves expression.

**5. Your Weakness Will Become Angry When It Is Ignored.** Rejection unleashes a battle.

**6. Your Weakness Has Cousins.** It will not rest until every one of them comes to visit and replaces a void in your life. The adultery of David birthed the murder of Uriah. (Read 2 Samuel 11:1-17.)

**7. Your Weakness Is Always An Enemy To Thankfulness.** You see, you are never thankful for a Weakness. Weakness is unappreciated. It reacts vehemently and begins a relentless journey to choke out any sign of thankfulness. Your Weakness knows you hate it. It never receives the praise, adoration and recognition that your strength receives.

## *Your Weakness Can Destroy You*

**1. Your Weakness Separates You From The Right People.** Adam withdrew from God in the garden after he sinned. "And they heard the voice of the Lord God walking in the garden in the cool of the day: and Adam and his wife hid themselves from the presence of the Lord God amongst the trees of the garden," (Genesis 3:8).

**2. Your Weakness Is The Entry Point For Satan And Demonic Spirits.** Satan entered Judas. "Jesus answered, He it is, to whom I shall give a sop, when I have dipped it. And when He had dipped the sop, He gave it to Judas Iscariot, the son of Simon," (John 13:26).

**3. Your Weakness Will Not Remain In You Alone But Will Move Toward Others And Infect Those Around You.** It will become bigger and bigger, stronger and stronger. It considers you, your dreams and future to be its greatest enemy.

**4. Your Weakness Has An Agenda, A Plan To Take Over Your Life And Sabotage It.** "Then when lust hath conceived, it bringeth forth sin: and sin, when it is finished, bringeth forth death," (James 1:15).

**5.    Your Weakness Despises The Exploits And Accomplishments of Your Strength.**  "And Delilah said to Samson, Tell me, I pray thee, wherein thy great strength lieth, and wherewith thou mightest be bound to afflict thee," (Judges 16:6).

**6.    Your Weakness Must Be Destroyed, Not Tolerated And Enjoyed Occasionally.**    God instructed King Saul to destroy all the Amalekites *completely*.  He ignored the instruction and suffered the consequences.  "And Saul smote the Amalekites from Havilah until thou comest to Shur, that is over against Egypt.  And he took Agag the king of the Amalekites alive, and utterly destroyed all the people with the edge of the sword.  But Saul and the people spared Agag, and the best of the sheep, and of the oxen, and of the fatlings, and the lambs, and all that was good, and *would not utterly destroy them:* but every thing that was vile and refuse, that they destroyed utterly," (1 Samuel 15:7-9).

**7.    Your Weakness Hates Your Strengths.**  You see, your strengths are a threat to your Weakness.

## *Your Weakness Is The War of Your Life*

**1.    The War of Your Life Is Between Your Strength And Your Weakness.**    "For the flesh lusteth against the Spirit, and the Spirit against the flesh:  and these are contrary the one to the other:  so that ye cannot do the things that ye would," (Galatians 5:17).

**2.    Everyone Has A Weakness.** "For all have sinned," (Romans 3:23).

**3.    Your Weakness Can Emerge At Any Time In Your Life, Including Your Closing Years.**

"Cast me not off in the time of old age; forsake me not when my strength faileth," (Psalm 71:9).

   **4.   Your Weakness Searches For Every Opportunity To Grow.** (Read Matthew 6:22-23.)

   **5.   What Others May Not Consider A Weakness, God Knows Is Your Weakness.** Your conscience confirms it, too.

   **6.   Every Weakness Grows.** It cannot stay the same. It is being fed and nourished or destroyed and starved. "Your glorying is not good. Know ye not that a little leaven leaveneth the whole lump?" (1 Corinthians 5:6).

   **7.   Your Weakness Has A Will of Its Own.** "I find then a law, that, when I would do good, evil is present with me," (Romans 7:21).

   **8.   Nobody Has Merely One Weakness.** Your strongest Weakness invites another one to come and visit. Exaggeration births lying.

   Your Weakness is not a whimpering puppy to be fed when hungry. Your Weakness is a deadly, rabid wolf to be *despised, rejected* and *destroyed.*

   Do not make friends with your Weakness. Do not bond with it.

   *Become An Enemy To Your Weakness.*

   This is One of the Secrets to becoming an Uncommon Leader.

RECOMMENDED INVESTMENTS:
Seeds of Wisdom on Overcoming, Vol. 5 (Book/B-17/32 pages)
Seeds of Wisdom on Enemies, Vol. 22 (Book/B-124/32 pages)
Seeds of Wisdom on Motivating Yourself, Vol. 31
   (Book/B-171/32 pages)
**Order Online Today..! MikeMurdockBooks.com**

# ❧ 20 ❧

# NEVER MAKE IMPORTANT DECISIONS WHEN YOU ARE TIRED

*Tired Eyes Rarely See A Great Future.*

When I am weary, I am not the same person. I do not have the same kind of faith, the same kind of enthusiasm and the same kind of patience as I do when I am rested, strengthened and feeling good in my spirit.

## *When You Are Tired...*

**1. Mountains Look Bigger.** I do not understand it...but it is true. When I am tired at night, things that normally would appear simple suddenly feel very burdensome and complex. Tasks that usually require a minimal effort suddenly seem too much to take on.

**2. Valleys Seem Deeper.** Discouraging factors seem to enlarge. Disappointments seem keener and stronger when my body is worn out.

**3. Offenses Come Easier.** I seem more offended than I normally would be. Little things become big.

When I am tired, I begin to replay over in my mind wrongs that people have done to me.

When I am rested, my mind moves to positive, wonderful and glorious dreams...things I want to accomplish and do.

Fatigue affects me in the opposite manner.

Jesus understood this. That is why He encouraged His disciples to, "Come ye yourselves apart into a desert place, and rest a while," (Mark 6:31). One of our great presidents once said that he would never make a decision past 3:00 in the afternoon. He was too tired and weary to consider every option available.

**4. You Become Less Tolerant of The Views And Needs of Others.** When others are weary, they seem less understanding of your own opinions and views, also.

**5. Your Focus Is More On What You Want Instead of The Appropriate Method For Achieving It.** You can get what you want but lose what you have. Many, in pursuit of riches, have lost their family through neglecting them.

**6. Your Focus Turns To Short-Term Goals Rather Than Long-Term Goals.** Wisdom is simply thinking ahead. The wiser you are, the further ahead you plan.

**7. Your Words Become Rash, Hasty And Usually Inappropriate.** One contentious conversation can destroy a 20 year friendship.

**8. You Become Unwilling To Invest Appropriate And Sufficient Time For Planning Ahead On A Project.**

**9. You Begin To Meditate On Your Own Mistakes And The Mistakes of Others.** There is a Scripture that indicates that satan wants to wear out the saints. *I believe that.* "And he shall speak great words against the most High, and shall wear out the saints of the most High, and think to change times and laws: and they shall be given into his hand until a time and times and the dividing of time," (Daniel 7:25).

Rest will restore.

*Never make important decisions unless you are strengthened, mentally alert and spiritually perceptive.*

*Never Make Important Decisions When You Are Tired.*

This is One of the Secrets to becoming an Uncommon Leader.

**RECOMMENDED INVESTMENTS:**
Seeds of Wisdom on Warfare, Vol. 7 (Book/B-19/32 pages)
Seeds of Wisdom on Motivating Yourself, Vol. 31
  (Book/B-171/32 pages)
**Order Online Today..! MikeMurdockBooks.com**

Anything You Do Not Have Is
Stored In Someone Near You,
And Love Is The Secret
Map To The Treasure.

-MIKE MURDOCK

# 21

# IDENTIFY WHAT YOU POSSESS THAT OTHERS NEED

*Everyone Has Problems.*

*Someone needs you desperately.* "Greater love hath no man than this, that a man lay down his life for his friends," (John 15:13).

Your success and happiness in life depend on your willingness to help someone solve their problem. *Successful people are simply problem-solvers.* A successful attorney solves *legal* problems. Doctors solve *physical* problems. The automobile mechanic solves *car* problems.

## Jesus Is Our Perfect Example

Jesus was a *Problem-Solver.*

Thousands were burdened with guilt because of their sins. Jesus offered *forgiveness.* Thousands were spiritually starved. He said, "I am the Bread of Life." Hundreds had bodies riddled with sickness and disease. Jesus "went about doing good, and healing all that were oppressed of the devil; for God was with Him," (Acts 10:38). Many were possessed with evil spirits. Jesus set them free.

*Jesus had something others needed.*

He solved their problems. That is why thousands sat for days as He taught them concerning the laws of God and how to have extraordinary relationships with other people.

His products were boldly declared...eternal life...
joy...inner peace...forgiveness...healing and health...
financial freedom. Take an inventory of yourself.
What do you have to offer someone? What do you
enjoy doing? *What would you attempt to do if you
knew it was impossible to fail?*

## You Are Irreplaceable In Your Assignment

Jonah revealed this when God used winds and a
huge fish to motivate him. Nobody was chosen to
"replace" him.

You are not an accident. God planned your birth.
"Before I formed thee in the belly I knew thee; and
before thou camest forth out of the womb I sanctified
thee, and I ordained thee a prophet unto the nations,"
(Jeremiah 1:5).

*Everything God makes is a solution to a problem.*
Every person God created is a solution to a problem.
God wanted a love relationship...He created Adam.
Adam was lonely...God created Eve. This is the
golden thread that links creation.

Think of your contribution to another as an
*Assignment* from God. A lawyer is *assigned* to his
client. A wife is *assigned* to her husband. Parents are
*assigned* to their children. A secretary is *assigned* to
her boss.

*Your Assignment is always to a person or a people.*
For example, Moses was assigned to the
Israelites. Aaron was assigned to Moses.

*Your Assignment will always solve a problem.*
Your life is a solution to someone in trouble. Find
those who need you. Discover what you have to offer.

*Build your life around that contribution.*

# 13 Qualities of Uncommon Leaders Distinguish Themselves In Their Assignment

1.    Uncommon Leaders Hear What Others Do Not Hear.

2.    Uncommon Leaders See What Others Do Not See.

3.    Uncommon Leaders Say What Others Do Not Want To Say.

4.    Uncommon Leaders Go Where Others Are Afraid To Go.

5.    Uncommon Leaders Think What Others Do Not Take The Time To Think.

6.    Uncommon Leaders Give People What They Need Instead of What They Want, When They Do Not Really Think They Need It.

7.    Uncommon Leaders Allow Time For Changes.

8.    Uncommon Leaders Believe In People And Their Uniqueness.

9.    Uncommon Leaders Care.

10.  Uncommon Leaders Dream Aloud.

11.  Uncommon Leaders Energize Others.

12.  Uncommon Leaders Focus On Real Issues.

13.  Uncommon Leaders Grow.

*Identify What You Possess That Others Need.*

This is One of the Secrets to becoming an Uncommon Leader.

What You Can Tolerate
You Cannot Change.

*-MIKE MURDOCK*

# 22

# LEARN FROM UNHAPPY VOICES AROUND YOU

*Unhappy People Birth Uncommon Ideas.*

Biographies of great businesses typically include a record of customer complaints. Those complaints created changes, correction and ultimately, uncommon profits. I often read success suggestions from uncommon entrepreneurs. Every extraordinary business champion states clearly, *"Listen to your customers. They will tell you the problems that require solving."*

I will never forget the teaching of one of the most respected minister friends in my life: "Listen to happy voices for encouragement. Listen to unhappy voices for ideas."

## 5 Important Keys

**1. Joseph Understood The Secret of Studying The Unhappy.** It was the secret of his promotion to the palace. Compassion was his dominant gift. When he noticed the downcast faces of two prisoners, he inquired and pursued an explanation. The butler and baker for Pharaoh explained their dreams. Joseph interpreted those dreams accurately. Two years later, Joseph was remembered by the butler for responding to his sorrowful countenance and dream. Joseph became the prime minister within 24 hours.

▶ You need *encouraging* voices to strengthen you.

▶ You need *mentoring* voices to avoid mistakes.

▶ You need *unhappy* voices for creativity and ideas.

*Listening Is The Vehicle To Solutions.*

**2.    Never Assume You Understand The Real Cause of Sorrows, Despondency or Anger Within Others.** Let me explain. I dearly loved a young couple that worked for me. Continuously, I looked for ways to bless them and encourage them. Occasionally, I would press a large bill in his hand at the airport and say, "Take your wife out to supper tonight." Yet, their agitation persisted. Nothing was ever enough for them. After much thought, listening and studying of their life, I discovered the following elements:

▶ They refused pastoral mentorship and faithful attendance to a local church.

▶ They refused to follow the principles of success that I taught them privately.

▶ They refused to attend sessions on financial prosperity held within minutes of their home.

**3.    Never Attempt To Solve The Problems of The Unteachable.** The unteachable always remain unhappy. That is why Jesus never pursued Pharisees. He never visited them when they were sick. Jesus went where He was desired, not where He was needed.

**4. Do Not Invest More Time In The Unhappy Than You Do Those Who Are Supportive And Encouraging To You.** Too often, those who bless us are ignored. The satisfied are overlooked. The obnoxious often receive far too much time, energy and attention. Be sensitive. That is why Jesus never gave long answers to Pharisees. He saved His time for Zacchaeus and the woman at the well... those who qualified for The Seed of His attention.

**5. It Is Not Your Responsibility To Solve Every Problem For Everyone Around You.** Jesus did not try. You cannot do it. You are human. Accept that. Do only what you are instructed by The Holy Spirit to do.

*Learn From Unhappy Voices Around You.*

I learned this from one of the most effective teachers I have ever known, Pastor Sherman Owens of Sarasota, Florida.

This is One of the Secrets to becoming an Uncommon Leader.

Those Who Do Not
Respect Your Time
Will Not Respect
Your Wisdom Either.

-MIKE MURDOCK

# ～ 23 ～

# ALWAYS HONOR THE FOCUS AND SCHEDULE OF OTHERS

*Respect The Focus of Others.*

I had finished a two-day School of The Holy Spirit up north. It had been a glorious two days. The presence of God was so powerful. I loved being with my friends and partners, as always.

However, due to the airline schedule, I had to leave 30 minutes earlier than planned. Another minister was going to finish the session for me. Because of the airline schedule, two flights were necessary and would let me arrive at my destination approximately at 1:00 a.m. My schedule was hectic. In fact, I would barely make the church where I was scheduled. So, I *announced* to everyone present that my plane schedule was tight. I would be unable to stay afterwards for any additional conversation.

Yet, as I was rushing toward the door with my briefcase, my associate by my side, 5 to 7 people stopped me. Standing in front of me, they insisted that I autograph my books. Some insisted that I hear about an experience they had had. Each one of them *totally ignored my own schedule.* They had no concern whatsoever.

Did they love me? Not really. They loved *themselves.* Their only obsession was *to get something* they wanted, regardless of the toll it took on me. My needs meant nothing.   My own schedule was unimportant to them.

## *5 Facts In Honoring Your Sensitivity To Others' Time*

**1.    The Holy Spirit Is Always Offended By Insensitivity And Uncaring For Others.**   "In honour preferring one another," (Romans 12:10).

**2.    Always Mark Those Who Show Disregard And Disrespect For Your Time, The Most Precious Gift God Gave You.**  If they do not respect your time, neither will they respect your Wisdom.

**3.    Always Make Sure Your Time With Someone Is Appropriate For Their Schedule.** (Read Ecclesiastes 3:1-8.)

**4.    Reject Manipulating, Intimidating And Abusive Words.**  "You never take time for me," is simply an attempt to manipulate you.   Statements like, "You never have time for me.  You always have time for everyone else," is victim vocabulary.   This kind of person has no true regard for others. They are obsessed with *themselves*.   You cannot give them enough time or attention to satisfy them.

**5.    When You Honor The Schedule of Others, Favor Will Follow.**

*Always Honor The Focus And Schedule of Others.*

This is One of the Secrets to becoming an Uncommon Leader.

# ≈ 24 ≈

# MENTOR THE INEXPERIENCED AROUND YOU WILLINGLY

*You Will Always Remember What You Teach.*

"Give instruction to a wise man, and he will be yet wiser: teach a just man, and he will increase in learning," (Proverbs 9:9).

Someone has said that you do not learn anything when you talk; that you only learn when you listen. *That* is inaccurate. Some of my greatest thoughts and ideas have surfaced while I was teaching others.

It is very important that you mentor others. Train them. Teach them what you know...especially those whom you have authority over; any person who is carrying out an instruction from you...employees, children or whomever.

Successful businesses have employees who are informed, well-trained and confident about carrying out their instructions. This takes time. It takes energy. It takes great patience.

Every song needs a singer. Every achiever needs motivation. Every student needs a teacher.

## *Jesus Was A Master Teacher*

He *taught* thousands at a time. Sometimes, He sat with His 12 disciples and fed information into them. He kept them motivated, influenced and inspired.

He *taught* them about *prayer*. (See Matthew 26:36-46.) He *taught* them about *Heaven*. (See John 14:2-4.) He *taught* them about *hell*. (See Luke 16:20-31.) He *educated* His staff on many topics including His death, giving and relationships.

Jesus *taught* in synagogues. (See Luke 13:10.) He also *taught* in the villages. (See Mark 6:6.)

Here is the point. None of us were born with great knowledge. You *became* what you are. You *discovered* what you know; it took time, energy and learning.

*Your staff will not know everything.* They may not see what you see. They may not feel what you feel. They may not have discovered what you know. You must invest time to nurture their vision, their product knowledge and the rewards you want them to pursue.

You need *good* people around you. You need *inspired* people around you. You need *informed* people around you. You may be their *only* source for information and motivation.

Make DVDs for them.

Create a standardized response for them. Document through video or DVD your expectations, procedures and desires.

Jesus educated His staff. Jesus constantly motivated the people He led by showing them the future of their present commitment.

*Take the time to train others.*

*Mentor The Inexperienced Around You Willingly.*

This is One of the Secrets to becoming an Uncommon Leader.

# ⚘ 25 ⚘

# ALWAYS ALLOW OTHERS ROOM TO TURN AROUND

*Everybody Makes Mistakes.*

Everybody deserves the chance to change; *allow them to do so.*

When pressure increases, those around you are affected and influenced. Their stress can affect you. The constant demands of others often birth impatience and mistakes. During these moments, *your mercy* is necessary.

Wrong words are often blurted out. Inaccurate assessments are made resulting in wrong decisions.

Think back upon your own life. Many frustrations drove you to that moment of indiscretion...those cutting words and angry outbursts.

## *What You Can Sow Into Others*

***Allow Forgiveness.*** Do not force others to live by their past bad decisions. *Whatever* you sow will come back to you a hundred times. Give them space to come back into the relationship *with dignity.* Jesus taught it. "Blessed are the merciful: for they shall obtain mercy," (Matthew 5:7).

***Forgive Them 490 Times.*** "Then came Peter to Him, and said, Lord, how oft shall my brother sin against me, and I forgive him? till seven times? Jesus saith unto him, I say not unto thee, Until seven times: but, Until seventy times seven," (Matthew 18:21-22). *Forgive 70 times 7.* Give them enough time. *Things are happening you cannot see.* Sometimes it takes weeks and even months for some to realize and admit their mistakes.

***Give Them A Season of Solitude.***

***Give Them Opportunities.*** They need an opportunity for *expression*...an opportunity to explain themselves. They may not know the right choice of words the first time. *Be willing to listen longer.*

***Give Them Time.*** They need time to evaluate every part of the puzzle. You may be looking at one part. They are considering many different factors they have yet to discuss with you.

***Give Them More Information About You.*** They need time to discover the truth about *you.* You already know yourself. *They do not.* They do not know all of your flaws. They do not know all of your capabilities. They do not understand your memories... your pain...your goals or dreams.

They may be looking at *now.* You are looking at *tomorrow.*

Allow others space to correct their mistakes.

*Always Allow Others Room To Turn Around.*

This is One of the Secrets to becoming an Uncommon Leader.

# ❧ 26 ❧

# OFFER INCENTIVES TO REWARD THOSE WHO HELP YOU ACHIEVE YOUR DREAMS

*Reward Those Who Help You Succeed.*

"And, behold, I come quickly; and my reward is with me, to give every man according as his work shall be," (Revelation 22:12).

People are motivated by two forces: pain or pleasure...fear or reward...loss or gain.

For example, you may ask your child to mow the lawn. He sulks and complains, "But Daddy, I do not really want to mow the lawn today. I want to go play with my friends."

You have two ways to motivate him: pain or pleasure...fear or incentive...loss or gain. For instance you may say, "Then son, bend over. I will have to discipline you with my belt." That is the pain motivation.

Or, you may use the *reward system.* "Son, I know you do not feel like doing it, but if you do it, I will pay you $10." That is incentive...reward...gain.

*Jesus used both methods to motivate.*

Jesus used fear motivation on Pharisees who ridiculed Him. He described to them how the rich man went to hell and was "tormented in this flame," (Luke 16:24).

However, when Jesus was talking to His disciples, He used *rewards* and *incentives* to motivate them. "In My Father's house are many mansions: if it were not so, I would have told you. I go to prepare a place for you," (John 14:2).

You are created with a desire to *increase*. *Decrease is unnatural.* Remember, every person you meet today has an *appetite for increase.* They want to be benefited. There is nothing wrong with that. There is a God-given command on the inside of each person...to become more. To *multiply.* (See Genesis 1:28.)

Carefully examine the benefits that you offer to others. Who *needs* your product? Why do they need it? What *problem* will your product *solve in their life?* What do you offer others that they cannot find anywhere else?

*Study the incentives* of your present business. Know them thoroughly. Incidentally, people never buy your product for the reasons you sell it. They buy products for what it will *do for them.*

## Uncommon Leaders Are Reward-Motivated

David asked what rewards would come to him if he killed the giant, Goliath. He was simply told that he would never have to pay taxes again, and he would be able to marry the king's daughter. He took 5 stones. He killed the giant. He had *motivation*. He had *incentive*.

People do things for different reasons. Interrogate; interview people. Ask questions. Find out what their greatest needs are. *Dig* to discover what their greatest fears may be.

Remember, you are there to *solve a problem*. Take the time to show others "what is in it for them." Make sure they understand the rewards and benefits of conducting business with you.

*Offer Incentives To Reward Those Who Help You Achieve Your Dreams.*

This is One of the Secrets to becoming an Uncommon Leader.

Favor Is
The Golden Bridge
From Your Pit
To Your Palace.

*-MIKE MURDOCK*

# ❧ 27 ❧

# LOOK FOR EVERY OPPORTUNITY TO SOW FAVOR

━━━━━▶▪◦◦◀━━━━━

*Favor Is Your Seed Into Others.*
Favor is the Divine current that takes you from your present season into your future dream.
*Favor is the Golden Bridge from your Pit to your Palace.*

## *10 Facts About Favor*

**1. Favor Is Someone's Desire To Solve A Problem For You.** Your own attitude determines God's attitude toward you. Follow the path of favor *wherever* it is happening in your life today. Who has discerned your worth? Who feels *kindly* toward your life? Who has been the source *most used* by God in your financial life within the last 12 months? Who has been your greatest source of spiritual *encouragement* and maturity? Who does God seem to be using *right now to open appropriate doors* for your life? Who is the *golden connection* that could easily shorten the trip that you have been taking toward your dream?

Recognize the *path*.

Recognize the *person*.

God is presently using them for this season. Stop evaluating their flaws. Stop building walls of distrust. Is God using them in your own life right now?

**2.    Favor Is A Gift From God.**  He does not owe it to you.  You cannot purchase favor.  Others are not obligated to you.  (When you obligate others, you create a potential enemy.  Those acts are called favors, not favor.)    "And to the angel of the church in Philadelphia write; These things saith He that is holy, He that is true, He that hath the key of David, He that openeth, and no man shutteth; and shutteth, and no man openeth," (Revelation 3:7).

**3.    Favor Is Necessary For Uncommon Success.**    You cannot work hard enough to get everything you deserve and want.  You cannot work enough jobs to generate the finances you will need for all your dreams and goals.  Others owe you nothing.  Yet, favor is necessary for you to take giant leaps into your future.  "Seven days shalt thou keep a solemn feast unto the Lord thy God in the place which the Lord shall choose:  because the Lord thy God shall bless thee in all thine increase, and in all the works of thine hands, therefore thou shalt surely rejoice," (Deuteronomy 16:15).

**4.    Favor Begins When You Solve A Problem For Someone.**  When Joseph interpreted the dream for Pharaoh, his gift made room for him.  He was promoted to the second place of power, prime minister.  "And Pharaoh took off his ring from his hand, and put it upon Joseph's hand, and arrayed him in vestures of fine linen, and put a gold chain about his neck; And he made him to ride in the second chariot which he had; and they cried before him, Bow the knee:  and he made him ruler over all the land of Egypt. And Pharaoh said unto Joseph, I am Pharaoh, and without thee shall no man lift up his hand or foot in all the land of Egypt," (Genesis 41:42-44).

**5.** **Favor Is A Seed You Can Sow Into Others.** *Everyone has the ability to sow favor.* Solving problems are Seeds of favor. Enabling others to succeed reveals favor. When you help others achieve their goals, you are sowing favor. "Knowing that whatsoever good thing any man doeth, the same shall he receive of the Lord, whether he be bond or free," (Ephesians 6:8).

*Favor begins as a Seed and ends as a Harvest.* What you sow today will re-enter your life in your future. This is the Harvest of favor. "Be not deceived; God is not mocked: for whatsoever a man soweth, that shall he also reap," (Galatians 6:7).

**6.** **Favor Can Stop When You Deliberately Ignore An Instruction From God.** Saul ignored the instructions of Samuel to kill King Agag, and all the Amalekites. Favor stopped. God altered the monarchy and David became king. "But Saul and the people spared Agag, and the best of the sheep, and of the oxen, and of the fatlings, and the lambs, and all that was good, and would not utterly destroy them: but every thing that was vile and refuse, that they destroyed utterly. Then came the word of the Lord unto Samuel, saying, It repenteth Me that I have set up Saul to be king: for he is turned back from following Me, and hath not performed my commandments. And it grieved Samuel; and he cried unto the Lord all night. And Samuel said unto Saul, I will not return with thee: for thou hast rejected the word of the Lord, and the Lord hath rejected thee from being king over Israel," (1 Samuel 15:9-11, 26).

Nebuchadnezzar experienced Uncommon

Success. When he became filled with pride, God let him become like a beast in the field for 7 years. "But when his heart was lifted up, and his mind hardened in pride, he was deposed from his kingly throne, and they took his glory from him: And he was driven from the sons of men; and his heart was made like the beasts, and his dwelling was with the wild asses: they fed him with grass like oxen, and his body was wet with the dew of Heaven; till he knew that the most high God ruled in the kingdom of men, and that He appointeth over it whomsoever He will," (Daniel 5:20-21).

**7. Favor Stops When The Tithe Is Withheld From God.** A curse comes instead of a blessing. "Will a man rob God? Yet ye have robbed me. But ye say, Wherein have we robbed Thee? In tithes and offerings. Ye are cursed with a curse: for ye have robbed Me, even this whole nation," (Malachi 3:8-9).

**8. Favor Can Make You Wealthy In One Day.** The peasant, Ruth, became the wife of the wealthy Boaz. "So Boaz took Ruth, and she was his wife: and when he went in unto her, the Lord gave her conception, and she bare a son," (Ruth 4:13).

**9. Favor Can Stop A Tragedy Instantly.** Favor prevents tragedies. It moved Joseph from the prison to the palace in 24 hours. "And Pharaoh said unto Joseph, Forasmuch as God hath shewed thee all this, there is none so discreet and wise as thou art: Thou shalt be over my house, and according unto thy word shall all my people be ruled: only in the throne will I be greater than thou," (Genesis 41:39-40). When Jonah cried out on the streets of Nineveh, favor flowed. God had sent Jonah to warn the Ninevites.

When the king called a fast, the favor of God was birthed. (See Jonah 3:10.)

**10. Favor Can Grow.** Jesus grew in favor with God and man. (See Luke 2:52.) The good happening of your today can increase 100 times within the next 12 months. "Then Peter began to say unto Him, Lo, we have left all, and have followed Thee. And Jesus answered and said, Verily I say unto you, There is no man that hath left house, or brethren, or sisters, or father, or mother, or wife, or children, or lands, for My sake, and the gospel's, But he shall receive an hundredfold now in this time, houses, and brethren, and sisters, and mothers, and children, and lands, with persecutions; and in the world to come eternal life," (Mark 10:28-30).

*Look For Every Opportunity To Sow Favor.*

This is One of the Secrets to becoming an Uncommon Leader.

When You Want Something
You Have Never Had,
You Have Got To Do Something
You Have Never Done.

*-MIKE MURDOCK*

# ❧ 28 ❧

# REMEMBER THAT WHEN YOU WANT SOMETHING YOU HAVE NEVER HAD, BE WILLING TO DO SOMETHING YOU HAVE NEVER DONE

*Everything Is Difficult At First.*

An Uncommon Leader refuses to stay in the Comfort Zone. The greatness of Abraham first surfaced when a Divine instruction came to leave his Comfort Zone. "Now the Lord had said unto Abram, Get thee out of thy country, and from thy kindred, and from thy father's house, unto a land that I will shew thee: And I will make of thee a great nation, and I will bless thee, and make thy name great; and thou shalt be a blessing," (Genesis 12:1-2).

When you were beginning to crawl, it was very difficult. When you took your first step, and fell...*that* was difficult.

*Thousands will fail in life because they are unwilling to make changes.* They refuse to change jobs, towns or friendships. They stay in comfort zones. Yet, thousands of others move up the ladder of happiness because they are willing to go through a little discomfort to experience a new level in life.

Peter wanted to walk on water. Jesus saw his excitement. He gave a simple instruction to Peter to do something he had never done before. "And he said, Come. And when Peter was come down out of the ship, he walked on the water, to go to Jesus," (Matthew 14:29).

*Jesus always gave people something to do.* And, it was always something *they had never done before.* He knew that their obedience was the only proof of their faith in Him.

Consider the instructions to the Israelites to march around the walls of Jericho 7 days in a row, and then 7 times on the seventh day. (Read Joshua 6.)

Consider the prophet's instructions to a leper to dip in the Jordan River 7 times for healing. (Read 2 Kings 5.)

Ruth left her home country of Moab to be with Naomi; she met Boaz who changed her life forever.

Elijah stretched the faith of the widow who was down to her last meal...two pancakes before death. He motivated her to do something she had never done—sow her Seed in expectation of a Harvest during famine. She saw the miracle come to pass. (Read 1 Kings 17.)

Jesus knew how to stretch people's faith. He motivated them. He helped them to do things they had never done before in order to create things they had never had.

*You, too, must be willing to do the unknown!*

*Ideas are Golden Gates to immediate change.*

An idea is a thought, Divinely planted by God, that could solve a problem for someone. The Scriptures excite us with the promise of "witty inventions." "I Wisdom dwell with prudence, and find out knowledge of witty inventions," (Proverbs 8:12).

*Methods for creating wealth are guaranteed to the obedient.* "But thou shalt remember the Lord thy God: for it is He that giveth thee power to get wealth, that He may establish His covenant which He sware unto thy fathers, as it is this day," (Deuteronomy 8:18).

Many years ago, I planted an incredible Seed in Columbus, Ohio. Six weeks later, I was in Houston, Texas, staying at the Hyatt Regency Hotel. It was Tuesday morning, 7:15 a.m., during my second hour of prayer. Suddenly, The Holy Spirit *birthed an idea.* I saw in my spirit a special Bible for mothers. It would contain 2,000 Scriptures to help mothers locate within 10 seconds the Scripture appropriate for solving an immediate problem they faced. I called it, *The Mother's Topical Bible.* Then, I saw one in my mind called, *The Father's Topical Bible* especially for fathers going through difficult places in their life.

Then *The Businessman's Topical Bible* exploded in my heart. Then, I saw one especially designed for teenagers who did not understand how to find Scriptures in the Bible...*The Teenager's Topical Bible.*

I called a friend in the publishing business. He was elated.

"Mike, we will print 60,000 leather-bound editions and see how they sell in the bookstores. You will receive a small royalty from each one that sells."

Within months, 1,300 bookstores purchased *every copy* of those Bibles. Eventually, paperbacks were printed. Different translations such as the Living Bible and New International Version were made available.

That *idea* unlocked hundreds of thousands of dollars. Someone told me that almost two million of those Topical Bibles have gone throughout the earth.

*That idea produced blessings for millions.*

I recognized it was from God. It was given to me. Yes, others have copied it and imitated it. It was a Divinely inspired idea God gave to me.

But, *I had to recognize it.*

Several years ago, while in prayer, The Holy Spirit gave me another little Bible idea. It is called the *One-Minute Pocket Bible.* Anyone can carry it in their shirt pocket. The small *One-Minute Pocket Bible* has gone throughout America. One of the greatest television ministries today purchased thousands for their partners. Every Mother's Day, pastors give these Pocket Bibles and Topical Bibles to ladies in their church.

*Good ideas are interesting but are not commands.*

*God ideas are actually God commands.* They awaken you in the middle of the night, becoming your obsession.

Oral Roberts once explained that when God promised you more than you *"have room to receive,"* He was speaking of ideas, insights and concepts. He instructed the people to review any idea, insight or concept God had given them and then present it to God for blessing.

One man listened with great faith. Years prior, he had had an idea. It was repeatedly rejected. He became demoralized and discouraged with it. He had stored it in boxes in his attic. After hearing Brother Roberts, he decided that the idea was from God. Satan had simply paralyzed his expectations and faith.

He went home, crawled into his attic and brought the boxes back down. Today, he is worth over one hundred million dollars...*because of that idea.*

Are you sitting on a million-dollar idea? Are you chasing pennies...when God gave you a million-dollar concept?

Years ago, I was speaking in Dothan, Alabama. When I finished preaching, I asked the people to give their Seed an Assignment as they planted The Seed in the offering.

"Write on your check where you most need to see your Harvest today," I instructed.

Some months later, I returned to the church. The pastor was exhilarated.

"I want you to meet this couple. Do you remember asking the people to give their Seed an Assignment? You told them to write on the check where they would like to see God produce their Harvest the most."

He explained that within 90 days from the time they had planted their Seed, an idea that had been ignored and rejected was suddenly accepted by a major grocery chain. Their *first* check for their first order was for *2.4 million dollars.*

*Their idea was worth 2.4 million dollars.*

Ross Perot, the famed billionaire, said *"One Good Idea Can Enable A Man To Live Like A King The Rest of His Life."*

*Enter* God's presence to receive His *commands.*

*Stay* in God's presence to receive His *plan.*

God is talking to you.

Are you listening?

## *8 Facts You Should Know About Ideas*

**1.    An Uncommon Idea Comes Through Observation of What Is Around You.**

**2.    An Uncommon Idea Will Help People.**

**3.    An Uncommon Idea From God Will Solve Problems For Somebody.**

**4.    An Uncommon Idea Is A Solution That Eliminates Stress, Increases Enthusiasm And Joy.**

**5.    An Uncommon Idea Can Come To You Whether It Is Respected By Those Around You or Not.**  Walt Disney was fired from a newspaper because he was "not creative enough."

**6.    An Uncommon Idea Can Create Uncommon Wealth.**

**7.    An    Uncommon    Idea    Requires Uncommon Attention.**

**8.    An Uncommon Idea Can Create A Lifetime of Provision.**

Recognition of a God-inspired idea that provides a lifetime income for your family.

*Remember That When You Want Something You Have Never Had, Be Willing To Do Something You Have Never Done.*

This is One of the Secrets to becoming an Uncommon Leader.

# ∼ 29 ∼

# KEEP A DIGITAL RECORDER WITH YOU AT ALL TIMES TO DOCUMENT IDEAS, INFORMATION AND INSTRUCTIONS

*Right Equipment And Technology Matter.*

Proper equipment increases your productivity.

Never have someone do a job that a machine can do instead. This is a humorous explanation of the advantages of proper machines.

## *10 Advantages In Using Appropriate Technology*

1. *Machines Do Not Require Coaxing, Just Repair.*

2. *Machines Do Not Get Discouraged When Their Mother-in-law Comes To Town.*

3. *Machines Are Never Disloyal, Discussing Your Secrets With Everyone Else.*

4. *Your Machines Will Not File Grievance Reports Against You When You Fail To Meet Their Expectations.*

5. *Machines Do Not Require Medical*

*Insurance, Sick Leave or Time Off.*

6. *Machines Can Be Replaced Quickly And Easily Without Breaking Your Heart.*

7. *Machines Do Not Request A Retirement Fund And Want To Be Paid For The Years Ahead When They Do Not Perform.*

8. *Machines Never Come To Work Late And Want To Leave Early.*

9. *Machines Will Work Through Lunch, Requiring No "Break Time."*

10. *Machines Never Interrupt The Productivity of Other Machines, Slowing Down The Entire Project.*

## 6 Qualities of True Leaders...They Will:

1. *Find The Most Effective Equipment Possible To Do Their Present Job.*

2. *Telephone Other Businesses or Companies To Locate Appropriate or Needed Machines And Equipment.*

3. *Attend Seminars And Workshops That Increase Their Efficiency or Skills On Computers And Other Machines.*

4. *Provide Their Team What Is Needed To Do The Job More Efficiently, More Accurately And Quickly.* (He will usually do anything possible to make the hours of employees more effective and productive.)

5. *Continuously Evaluate Their Work.* What is slowing them down? What machine could make a big difference in the completion of their daily tasks and responsibilities?

6. *Present Their Supervisors With Options, Costs And Potential Benefits of Purchasing More Machines.* Your staff will treasure it and learn to appreciate their own work load reduction because of it. It decreases the opportunities for mistakes. It increases their sense of progress and accomplishment.

Search for appropriate equipment to accomplish your tasks quickly. Never do what a machine can do.

*Keep A Digital Recorder With You At All Times To Document Ideas, Information And Instructions.*

This is One of the Secrets to becoming an Uncommon Leader.

Access Creates Demands;
    Demands Create Expectations;
Expectations Create Distraction;
    Distraction Creates Failure.

-MIKE MURDOCK

# ∽ 30 ∽
# IDENTIFY FOOLS QUICKLY AND DENY THEM ACCESS TO YOU AND ALL IMPORTANT INFORMATION

*The Wise Recognize Fools.*

Fools are everywhere. There are fools in the educational institution, in the world of religion, in the political arena and even among your relatives.

Fools break your focus.

Fools waste valuable time and energy.

Fools slow your life down.

Fools rob you of precious moments.

I mentioned a statement by former President Richard Nixon in one of my books, *Secrets of the Richest Man Who Ever Lived.* He commented that Lee Iacocca, the legendary leader of Chrysler, had one major problem—no tolerance for fools. Nixon further explained that his attitude created two more problems! First, there are so many fools and second, some people that you think are fools really are not!

## 43 Important Facts You Should Know About Fools

1.  **A Fool Is Anyone Who Despises Wisdom,**

**Instruction And Correction From A Proven Mentor.** "The fear of the Lord is the beginning of knowledge: but fools despise Wisdom and instruction," (Proverbs 1:7).

**2. A Fool Is Anyone Who Attempts To Destroy The Reputation of A Proven Champion Through Lying And Misrepresentation.** "He that uttereth a slander, is a fool," (Proverbs 10:18).

**3. A Fool Is Anyone Who Refuses To Depart From Evil, Even Though Corrected.** "But it is abomination to fools to depart from evil," (Proverbs 13:19).

**4. A Fool Is Anyone Who Does Not Take The Danger of Sin Seriously.** "Fools make a mock at sin: but among the righteous there is favour," (Proverbs 14:9).

**5. A Fool Is Anyone Who Reveals Confidences That Should Be Kept Private.** "Wisdom resteth in the heart of him that hath understanding: but that which is in the midst of fools is made known," (Proverbs 14:33).

**6. A Fool Is Any Son That Disregards The Wisdom of His Father.** "A fool despiseth his father's instruction: but he that regardeth reproof is prudent," (Proverbs 15:5).

**7. A Fool Is Any Son Who Shows Disrespect Toward The Mother That Brought Him Into The World.** "A wise son maketh a glad father: but a foolish man despiseth his mother," (Proverbs 15:20).

**8. A Fool Is Anyone Whose Conduct Does Not Change Even After Experiencing Painful**

**Consequences From It.** "A reproof entereth more into a wise man than an hundred stripes into a fool," (Proverbs 17:10).

**9. A Fool Is Anyone Who Considers Any Pursuit of Wisdom To Be A Wasted Effort.** "Wherefore is there a price in the hand of a fool to get Wisdom, seeing he hath no heart to it?" (Proverbs 17:16).

**10. A Fool Is Anyone Who Continually Expresses His Discontent With God.** "The foolishness of man perverteth his way: and his heart fretteth against the Lord," (Proverbs 19:3).

**11. A Fool Is Anyone Who Refuses To Embrace Peace.** "It is an honour for a man to cease from strife: but every fool will be meddling," (Proverbs 20:3).

**12. A Fool Is Any Man Who Spends More Money Than He Is Willing To Earn For His Family.** "There is treasure to be desired and oil in the dwelling of the wise; but a foolish man spendeth it up," (Proverbs 21:20).

**13. A Fool Is Anyone Who Creates His Own Belief System, Contrary To The Word of God.** "He that trusteth in his own heart is a fool: but whoso walketh wisely, he shall be delivered," (Proverbs 28:26).

**14. A Fool Is Anyone Who Refuses To Pay His Debts.** "When thou vowest a vow unto God, defer not to pay it; for He hath no pleasure in fools: pay that which thou hast vowed. Better is it that thou shouldest not vow, than that thou shouldest vow and not pay," (Ecclesiastes 5:4-5).

**15. A Fool Is Anyone Who Makes Financial Increase His Life Focus Rather Than God.** "But God said unto him, Thou fool, this night thy soul shall be required of thee: then whose shall those things be, which thou hast provided? So is he that layeth up treasure for himself, and is not rich toward God," (Luke 12:20-21).

**16. A Fool Is Someone Who Wants Something He Has Not Yet Earned.** Ahab's wife, Queen Jezebel, was also a fool. Her husband's bitter words concerning the man with the vineyard angered her heart. Why? She wanted something she had not yet earned.

**17. A Fool That Keeps Silent Often Remains Undetected.** "Even a fool, when he holdeth his peace, is counted wise: and he that shutteth his lips is esteemed a man of understanding," (Proverbs 17:28).

**18. A Fool Is Always At The Center of Strife And Contention.** "A fool's lips enter into contention, and his mouth calleth for strokes. A fool's mouth is his destruction, and his lips are the snare of his soul," (Proverbs 18:6-7).

**19. Any Companion of Fools Will Ultimately Be Destroyed.** "He that walketh with wise men shall be wise: but a companion of fools shall be destroyed," (Proverbs 13:20).

**20. The Wise Always Leave The Presence of Fools When They Perceive A Lack of Desire For Knowledge.** "Go from the presence of a foolish man, when thou perceivest not in him the lips of knowledge," (Proverbs 14:7).

**21. Liars Are Fools.** "He that hideth hatred with lying lips...is a fool," (Proverbs 10:18). A liar destroys his trustworthiness with a single sentence. He will trade a lifetime relationship for a single falsehood. Without a doubt, he is a fool.

**22. A Fool Is Usually Only Changed By Correction During His Childhood.** "Foolishness is bound in the heart of a child; but the rod of correction shall drive it far from him," (Proverbs 22:15).

**23. A Fool Cannot Be Changed Through Counsel.** "Speak not in the ears of a fool: for he will despise the Wisdom of thy words," (Proverbs 23:9).

**24. A Fool Should Never Be Given A Position of Leadership Over Others.** "Wisdom is too high for a fool: he openeth not his mouth in the gate," (Proverbs 24:7). In the ancient days, the wise elders of the city met at the gates of the city. Fools were never welcomed or given position of influence there.

**25. The Continuous Threat of Pain Is The Only Influence That Keeps A Fool In His Place.** "A whip for the horse, a bridle for the ass, and a rod for the fool's back," (Proverbs 26:3).

**26. A Fool Who Is Trusted Ultimately Destroys Those Who Trusted Him.** "He that sendeth a message by the hand of a fool cutteth off the feet, and drinketh damage," (Proverbs 26:6).

**27. A Fool Remains Unaffected or Changed By Any Wisdom He Quotes From Others.** "The legs of the lame are not equal: so is a parable in the mouth of fools," (Proverbs 26:7).

**28. A Fool, When Given A Position of Honor**

**or Power, Becomes Deadly To Those Within His Influence.** "As he that bindeth a stone in a sling, so is he that giveth honour to a fool," (Proverbs 26:8).

**29. Every Fool Will Eventually Taste The Consequences of His Attitude And Rebellion.** "The great God that formed all things both rewardeth the fool, and rewardeth transgressors," (Proverbs 26:10).

**30. A Fool Is Someone Who Makes The Same Mistakes Repeatedly.** "As a dog returneth to his vomit, so a fool returneth to his folly," (Proverbs 26:11).

**31. A Fool Uses His Anger To Threaten To Create Problems For Others.** "A stone is heavy, and the sand weighty; but a fool's wrath is heavier than them both," (Proverbs 27:3).

**32. A Fool Exposed Is More Destructive Than Wild Animals Disturbed.** "Let a bear robbed of her whelps meet a man, rather than a fool in his folly," (Proverbs 17:12).

**33. No Amount of Wisdom or Counsel Can Create A Peaceful Relationship With A Fool.** "If a wise man contendeth with a foolish man, whether he rage or laugh, there is no rest," (Proverbs 29:9).

**34. A Fool Tells Everything He Knows And Feels To Others.** "A fool uttereth all his mind: but a wise man keepeth it in till afterwards," (Proverbs 29:11).

**35. A Fool Talks Too Much And Is Known By His Torrent of Words.** "A fool also is full of words: a man cannot tell what shall be; and what shall be after him, who can tell him?" (Ecclesiastes 10:14). "A fool's voice is known by multitude of words,"

(Ecclesiastes 5:3).

**36. A Fool Never Believes That He Is Wrong.** "Keep thy foot when thou goest to the house of God, and be more ready to hear, than to give the sacrifice of fools: for they consider not that they do evil," (Ecclesiastes 5:1).

**37. The Parents of A Fool Will Live In Sorrow Their Entire Lifetime.** "He that begetteth a fool doeth it to his sorrow: and the father of a fool hath no joy," (Proverbs 17:21). "A foolish son is a grief to his father, and bitterness to her that bare him," (Proverbs 17:25).

**38. Any Atheist Is A Fool.** "The fool hath said in his heart, There is no God," (Psalm 14:1; see also Psalm 53:1).

**39. A Fool Does Not Learn From His Observation Nor Experiences Enough To Make Changes.** "Wisdom is before him that hath understanding; but the eyes of a fool are in the ends of the earth," (Proverbs 17:24).

**40. Any Conversation With Fools Should Be Avoided.** Association is defiling. Correction is useless. Solomon understood this. "Answer not a fool according to his folly, lest thou also be like unto him," (Proverbs 26:4). He refused to enter into any relationship or conversation.

**41. A Fool Perpetuates His Offenses To Others Around Him.** He wants others to feel his pain. He arouses an army of protesters against someone who offended him, rather than exhibiting a desire to settle the offense.

**42. A Fool Refuses To Admit His Mistakes Even When His Pain Is The Obvious Result.**

**43. A Fool Refuses To Reach For Counsel From Accessible Champions.** When I heard several complaints over financial problems, I offered to pay the registration to "The Uncommon Millionaire's Conference." I brought in 6 multi-millionaires to advise on financial blessing for 3 days. Those who had been complaining of their finances... never even attended the 21 hours of teaching at the conference, though some lived less than 5 minutes away.

Recognition of a fool will enable you to avoid a thousand heartbreaking experiences in your life.

*Identify Fools Quickly And Deny Them Access To You And All Important Information.*

This is One of the Secrets to becoming an Uncommon Leader.

RECOMMENDED INVESTMENT:
The Law of Recognition (Book/B-114/248 pages)
**Order Online Today..! MikeMurdockBooks.com**

# ☙ 31 ☙
# STANDARDIZE 7 DAILY SUCCESS RITUALS

━━━━◆▷·◉·◁◆━━━━

*Great Men Have Great Habits.*

In California, a powerful spiritual leader awakens at 5:30 a.m. each day. He has followed this routine for years. He prays from 5:30 to 6:30 a.m. *every morning* of his life. It is a *daily* habit—the success habit that has unlocked an unforgettable anointing for teaching. He walks, lives and breathes the atmosphere of *success.* Is it a mystery? Not really. When your Daily Success Routine begins with the first hour of every day in the presence of God, it is almost impossible to fail.

One of the most famous business women on earth lived here in Dallas, Texas. She was worth over 300 million dollars and her business is worth over 2 billion. She had a daily Success Routine. Since 1962, she would write her daily plan on a sheet of paper.

She listed only 6 tasks for the day.

She worked on the first, then the second, then the third, and so forth. She believed that one of The Master Keys to her uncommon success was this constant and consistent daily habit. *Planning was her daily routine.*

A former Presidential Chief-of-Staff revealed part of his Daily Success Routine. The *first* thing he did every morning and the *last* thing he did every night was to plan the day of the President. It was his habit.

One of the wealthiest athletes in history revealed a few weeks ago that the morning after he won the heavyweight championship of the world, he was back in his gym...his Daily Success Routine...the morning after! Millions of dollars were earned within minutes. But, he knew and had decided for his life, the *daily habits* necessary to create the *future* he loved.

One famous Hall of Fame baseball pitcher pitched his seventh no-hitter. Afterwards, reporters found him in the locker room doing what he always did—riding a stationary bike for one hour and fifteen minutes. He had just pitched a no-hitter! Did he race out and do something exciting and different? He did not become a champion by chasing after every thought fleeting through his mind. He became a champion through his Daily Success Routine. He had developed the *Habits for Greatness*.

Habit is the most misunderstood word in the English language. When someone talks about habits, everyone thinks about drugs, alcohol or smoking. They think habit is a word connected to something evil, deteriorating or deadly.

Habit is a good word, a powerful gift from God. Habit simply means that when you do something twice, it becomes easier. It is a gift from God enabling us to succeed.

*Personal hygiene habits* increase your health, self-confidence and social influence.

*Conversation habits* strengthen relationships, build confidence and integrity.

*Financial habits* can create uncommon increase.

Discipline is different than habit. God did not create us to be creatures of discipline but creatures of *habit.*

*The purpose of discipline is to birth a habit.*

Psychologists say that when you perform an act for 21 consecutive days without fail, it will become a habit.

Habits create a future you will love or hate.

*Habit is the child of purpose, destiny and desire.* Let me give you an example. When Mohammed Ali, the great boxer, believed that destiny and God had determined his future would be the greatest boxer on earth, his habits *changed.* He arose earlier. His workouts were more intense. His conversation changed. Yes, he even changed his name! You see, your habits are the result of your beliefs of what you truly believe you deserve to possess and have.

*Desires birth habits.* Some who have smoked for 40 years quit in a week when the doctor revealed that they were standing at the door of death.

Thirty years ago, I sat at the table of a pastor friend in Louisiana. I stared at him and asked, "How on earth did you become so huge?" (He weighed 400 pounds!)

"Eating every night after church just like you are eating right now," he said boldly.

I laughed. I thought he was simply a little peeved at my bluntness. But, he was sincere. (Unfortunately, I stayed ignorant!) What he really said to me was, "I have an eating routine. Every night, after I have spent a long day in work and effort, I sit at this table and comfort myself with food. *It is a habit in my life.* I didn't *begin* this big. It didn't happen within a few days. My habit of eating after church at night added a pound, another pound and another pound."

*Your habits have created your present physical condition.* Whether you are overweight, unhealthy or uncommonly strong, what you keep eating *daily* is creating the You-In-The-Future. What you eat is increasing your health or decreasing your health.

*Your spending habits are creating a secure financial future or destroying it completely.* A friend of mine told me that a simple saving of $100 invested in mutual funds, *every month*...would result in a baby becoming a millionaire at 20 years old. Just $100...monthly. Habits create paupers or millionaires.

## *Here Are 14 Wisdom Keys On Developing Your Daily Success Routine*

1. *Men Do Not Decide Their Future, They Decide The Habits That Determine Their Future.*

2. *What You Do Daily Is Deciding What You Are Becoming Permanently.*

3. *Nothing Will Ever Dominate Your Life Unless It Happens Daily.*

4. *You Cannot Change Your Life Until You Change Something You Keep Doing...Daily.*

5. *You Can Trace The Failure of Every Man To Something He Permitted To Occur Daily In His Life, Body or His Mind.*

6. *You Can Trace Uncommon Success To Habits That Were Created...A Daily Success Routine.*

7. *Your Habits Are Creating Increase or Decrease.*

8. *Your Habits Are Being Strengthened or Changed By The Friends You Permit Daily Close To You.*

9. *What You Keep Looking At Is Deciding Where You Will Go.*

10. *Gaze Only Upon That Which You Desire In Your Future.*

11. *You Will Always Move Toward The Dominant Picture In Your Mind.* That is why it is important that you place pictures around you of the things you desire to move toward and have.

12. *You Can Change A Failure Routine Into A Success Routine Within 21 Days.*

13. *What You Keep Doing Daily Is Creating The Future You Have Always Wanted or The Future You Dread.*

14. *Your Money Habits Are Making You A Pauper or A Millionaire.*

In the Ancient Writings, there are several photographs of people who had success habits and routines. Jesus went *regularly* to the synagogue. David prayed 7 *times* each day. Daniel prayed 3 *times* each day. Zacharias offered up sacrifices, as *was his custom.*

## *Here Are 7 Daily Habits I Have Recognized In The Lives of Uncommon Men And Women*

**1. Uncommon Leaders Arise At The Same Time Every Morning.** John R. Rice, the famous Baptist evangelist of many years ago, would often arrive home from his crusades at 3:00 or 4:00, on

Monday mornings. But his staff declared, "Regardless of when he arrived, he was at the office the same time each morning!"

**2. Uncommon Leaders Start Their Work At The Same Time Each Day.** One of my close friends told me, "The wealthiest man in our town backs out of his driveway at 7:55 every morning...without fail. Mike, I can set my clock by it." He has a Daily Success Routine.

Ernest Hemingway, the famed writer, wrote every night from midnight until 6:00 in the morning, then he would sleep from 6:00 a.m. to 2:00 in the afternoon. The most prolific writers in America have a Daily Success Routine, writing the same hours every day.

**3. Uncommon Leaders Pray At The Same Time Every Day.** David did. "Early will I seek Thee." Daniel prayed 3 times a day. Always establish a consistent appointment in The Secret Place. It will radically change your life. It may be for 5 minutes, but do it daily. It must become a part of your Daily Success Routine.

**4. Uncommon Leaders Read The Word of God Daily As A Part of Their Success Routine.** Reading 3 chapters a day (and 5 on Sundays) enables you to complete the Bible once a year. If you keep waiting until you have time, you will never read it. Your success routine in The Word will keep storing within you the thoughts and presence of God. *Nothing is more important than your appointment in The Secret Place each day reading The Word of God.*

My greatest success habit is *listening to the Bible every morning* on tape or CD when I awaken. It is the

THE UNCOMMON LEADER ■ 131

first thing I do every day even before I brush my teeth. His Word washes my mind, stimulates my faith, and puts a picture of my Best Friend before me, The Holy Spirit.

**5. Uncommon Leaders Habitually Speak Words of Hope, Confidence And Expectation of Excellence.** Words create your future.

Your words of faith and enthusiasm are the fuel unleashing the promised Harvest of your *Daily Success Routine.*

**6. Uncommon Leaders Have A Habit of Planning Their Day.** The late Mary Kay Ash, the famed multimillionaire, planned every day with a simple list of 6 things to do. Mark McCormack invests *one hour* every morning in planning the next 23 hours. Think about it! He plans his day for one solid hour before doing anything else.

**7. Uncommon Leaders Exercise Every Day of Their Life.** President Harry Truman walked an hour every day until he was almost 80 years old. He had determined the Daily Success Routine of his future.

> ► How passionate are you about your *Health?* You must create the Daily Success Routine that moves you toward that Harvest.
>
> ► How passionate are you about your *Wisdom?* You must include Mentorship every single day...as part of your Daily Success Routine.
>
> ► How passionate are you about *Finances?* You must invest time in creating a Daily Success Routine every day of your life...in

financial Mentorship, focus on an Uncommon Dream and strengthen the relationships that create increase...every day.

▶ How passionate are you in unleashing more *Favor* than you have ever known? You must *sow* Favor every single day...as a part of your Daily Success Routine.

When I began to meditate, read and study the Laws of Increase, many keys appeared: Tenacity, Integrity, Motivation and scores of others. When I determined to recognize the 7 most powerful keys, it exploded...The Daily Success Routine.

It has been ignored in most motivation books.

Now, what really causes a man to reverse the bad habits of his life and birth new ones? A tragedy in his life? A screaming mate? Not really. You simply have an awakening of a dormant, ignored, overlooked *Dream within you of how great your life can really become. You need a Dream.*

*An Uncommon Dream.*

▶ You cannot change your life until you change your *habits*.

▶ You cannot change your habits until you change your *Dream.*

▶ You will not change your Dream until you become angry with your present.

Are you feeling pain? You are ready for the Promised Harvest of Your Daily Success Routine.

I read an interesting statistic a few weeks ago in a powerful book on millionaires in America. It showed how the wealthiest people in America, by percentages, were people from *other countries* who entered the

United States *impoverished*. Their past was so painful and so powerful in their mind, they developed work and money habits that created incredible success. The book also explained how the middle-class American has almost no chance at wealth, *because he is not feeling enough pain.*

## *4 Important Facts You Should Know About Pain*

▶ Your pain determines your *motivation.*
▶ Your pain determines your *focus.*
▶ Your pain determines *who* you pursue.
▶ Your pain determines the Wisdom you believe is *worthy of pursuit.*

It will take more than a miracle anointing service, a self-help improvement book or a network marketing plan to unleash your *finances.*

It will take more than an exercise guru on television, a new jogging suit or a free membership at the gym...to unlock your *health.*

It will take more than 6 tapes from a marriage counselor, a bouquet of roses or a pretty negligee...to unlock more *passion* in your marriage.

It will require total focus on creating your Daily Success Routine.

*What You Keep Doing Daily Is Creating The Future You Have Always Wanted or The Future You Dread.*

When you change your daily routine, you can unlock the Promised Harvest for your family, your pastor and the work of God.

*Your Dream Is Deciding Your Habits.*

## *How To Create Your Daily Success Routine*

**1.    Recognize What Is Worthy of Your Total Focus Today.**  Everyone will have a different focus. You must target what you desire the most.  Permit others to stay in the center of their focus.

**2.    Pinpoint The Top 3 Distractions That Occur Habitually.**  *The Only Reason Men Fail Is Broken Focus.*  Satan cannot destroy you, merely *distract* you. You can trace any failure to loss of focus. What breaks your focus daily on the things you love the most?  Who can help you *protect* your focus?

**3.    Pray Continuously In The Holy Spirit.** He has an agenda.  You must discern His, not decide your own.

**4.    Determine The Core Product of Your Life.**  What do you want to do the most?  What is the *legacy* you desire to leave?  What are you willing to walk away from to see it take place?

*Everything does not have equal value.*

Everyone does not deserve equal time.

**5.    Embrace Flexibility As An Opportunity.** Hillary Rodham Clinton once said, "I've never had a plan yet where everything happened as I planned it." You can take advantage of the unexpected.

**6.    Recognize Those Around You Who Do Not Have A Determined Focus or Goal.**  They want your attention and do not hesitate to break your focus.

**7.    Discern Those Who Are Oblivious And Blind Toward Your Focus.**  I have been dictating books and have "friends" burst into the room distracting me with trivia. Confront rudeness.

**8.    Keep A Visual Picture of Your Desired Goal And Dream Before You.** Gyms have pictures of physical champions who have won Mr. USA, Miss America, and so forth, in front of them as motivation.

Abraham had a picture of the stars and the sand of the sea as personal motivation for his generations of children. Joseph had a picture of himself in authority. Jesus had a picture of returning to the Father.

**9.    Become Militant About Keeping Your Daily Success Routine.** One of the happiest seasons of my life was 12 years ago. I birthed a Daily Success Routine. I went to bed at 10:30 p.m. with a cup of hot chocolate. I arose at 5:30 and walked 3 miles in the morning and 3 miles at night. My joy was remarkable. My peace was unexplainable. After several weeks, a friend rushed into my hotel room. He wanted me to help him work on a special letter to his congregation and partners. I told him about my Daily Success Routine. It was late. I needed to sleep. He laughed it off and kept talking.

He finally left at 1:00 a.m.

My entire rhythm was affected. Quite deeply. I was unable to arise at 5:30 the next morning and pray, so I decided I would pray at 8:00 a.m. Every appointment the next day had to be changed. Something was lost that I cannot explain. It never came back for many, many months.

*A good habit is too powerful to treat lightly.* Become militant about keeping it.

*What You Look At The Longest Will Become The Strongest.*

## *10 Incredible Ways Words Can Affect Your Daily Success Rituals*

**1. Right Words Can Turn An Angry Man Into A Friend.** "A soft answer turneth away wrath," (Proverbs 15:1).

**2. Right Words Will Breathe Energy And Life Into Everything Around You.** "A wholesome tongue is a tree of life," (Proverbs 15:4).

**3. Right Words Can Energize And Motivate Your Own Life.** "A man hath joy by the answer of his mouth: and a word spoken in due season, how good is it!" (Proverbs 15:23).

**4. Right Words Decide Which Dreams Live And Which Dreams Die.** "Death and life are in the power of the tongue: and they that love it shall eat the fruit thereof," (Proverbs 18:21).

**5. Right Words Are As Important As Silver And Gold.** "The tongue of the just is as choice silver," (Proverbs 10:20).

**6. Right Words Can Get You Out of Trouble.** "...but the mouth of the upright shall deliver them," (Proverbs 12:6).

**7. Right Words Can Bring Health And Healing.** "...the tongue of the wise is health," (Proverbs 12:18).

**8. Right Words Can Open Doors To Powerful, Important And Influential Leaders.** "Righteous lips are the delight of kings; and they love him that speaketh right," (Proverbs 16:13).

**9. Right Words Can Cure Bitterness.** "Pleasant words are as an honeycomb, sweet to the soul, and health to the bones," (Proverbs 16:24).

**10. Right Words Can Unlock A Financial Raise or Promotion.** "A man's belly shall be satisfied with the fruit of his mouth; and with the increase of his lips shall he be filled," (Proverbs 18:20).

*Uncommon achievers place great importance on your ability to speak right words.* Dave Thomas, the beloved founder of Wendy's International, said in his book, *Well Done* (page 136), "Communication is the heart of success."

Your daily words affect your success.

*Standardize 7 Daily Success Rituals.*

This is One of the Secrets to becoming an Uncommon Leader.

# DECISION

## Will You Accept Jesus As Your Personal Savior Today?

The Bible says, "That if thou shalt confess with thy mouth the Lord Jesus, and shalt believe in thine heart that God hath raised Him from the dead, thou shalt be saved," (Romans 10:9).

Pray this prayer from your heart today!

*"Dear Jesus, I believe that You died for me and rose again on the third day. I confess I am a sinner...I need Your love and forgiveness...Come into my heart. Forgive my sins. I receive Your eternal life. Confirm Your love by giving me peace, joy and supernatural love for others. Amen."*

# DR. MIKE MURDOCK

is in tremendous demand as one of the most dynamic speakers in America today.

More than 23,000 audiences in over 133 countries have attended his Schools of Wisdom and conferences. Hundreds of invitations come to him from churches, colleges and business corporations. He is a noted author of over 900 books, including the best sellers, *The Leadership Secrets of Jesus* and *Secrets of the Richest Man Who Ever Lived*. Thousands view his weekly television program, *Wisdom Keys with Mike Murdock*. Many attend his Schools of Wisdom that he hosts in many cities of America.

*Clip and Mail*

☐ Yes, Mike, I made a decision to accept Christ as my personal Savior today. Please send me my free gift of your book, *31 Keys to a New Beginning* to help me with my new life in Christ.

NAME _____ BIRTHDAY _____

ADDRESS _____

CITY _____ STATE ____ ZIP _____

PHONE _____ EMAIL _____ **DFC**

*Mail to:* **The Wisdom Center** · 4051 Denton Hwy. · Ft. Worth, TX 76117
1-817-759-BOOK · 1-817-759-2665 · 1-817-759-0300
**MikeMurdockBooks.com**

138

## DR. MIKE MURDOCK

1 Has embraced his Assignment to Pursue...Proclaim...and Publish the Wisdom of God to help people achieve their dreams and goals.

2 Preached his first public sermon at the age of 8.

3 Preached his first evangelistic crusade at the age of 15.

4 Began full-time evangelism at the age of 19, which has continued since 1966.

5 Has traveled and spoken to more than 23,000 audiences in over 133 countries, including East and West Africa, Asia, Europe and South America.

6 Noted author of over 900 books, including best sellers, *Wisdom for Winning, Dream Seeds, The Double Diamond Principle, The Law of Recognition* and *The Holy Spirit Handbook.*

7 Created the popular *Topical Bible* series for Businessmen, Mothers, Fathers, Teenagers; *The One-Minute Pocket Bible* series, and *The Uncommon Life* series.

8 The Creator of the Master 7 Mentorship Program, an Achievement Program for Believers.

9 Has composed thousands of songs such as "I Am Blessed," "You Can Make It," "God Rides On Wings of Love" and "Jesus, Just The Mention of Your Name," recorded by many gospel artists.

10 Is the Founder and Senior Pastor of The Wisdom Center, in Fort Worth, Texas...a Church with International Ministry around the world.

11 Host of *Wisdom Keys with Mike Murdock,* a weekly TV Program seen internationally.

12 Has appeared often on TBN, CBN, BET, Daystar, Inspirational Network, LeSea Broadcasting and other television network programs.

13 Has led over 3,000 to accept the call into full-time ministry.

## THE MINISTRY

1 **Wisdom Books & Literature** - Over 900 best-selling Wisdom Books and 70 Teaching Tape Series.

2 **Church Crusades** - Multitudes are ministered to in crusades and seminars throughout America in "The Uncommon Wisdom Conferences." Known as a man who loves pastors, he has focused on church crusades for over 50 years.

3 **Music Ministry** - Millions have been blessed by the anointed songwriting and singing of Mike Murdock, who has made over 15 music albums and CDs available.

4 **Television** - *Wisdom Keys with Mike Murdock,* a nationally-syndicated weekly television program.

5 **The Wisdom Center** - The Church and Ministry Offices where Dr. Murdock speaks weekly on Wisdom for The Uncommon Life.

6 **Schools of The Holy Spirit** - Mike Murdock hosts Schools of The Holy Spirit in many churches to mentor believers on the Person and Companionship of The Holy Spirit.

7 **Schools of Wisdom** - In many major cities Mike Murdock hosts Schools of Wisdom for those who want personalized and advanced training for achieving "The Uncommon Dream."

8 **Missions Outreach** - Dr. Mike Murdock's overseas outreaches to over 133 countries have included crusades in East and West Africa, Asia, Europe and South America.

# 14 Harvests Are Waiting For You..!

Dear Friend,

### God has connected us!

I have asked The Holy Spirit for 3000 Special Partners who will plant a monthly Seed of $58.00 to help me bring the gospel around the world. (58 represents 58 kinds of blessings in the Bible.)

*Will you become my monthly Faith Partner in The Wisdom Key 3000?* Your monthly Seed of $58.00 is so powerful in helping heal broken lives. When you sow into the work of God, 4 Miracle Harvests are guaranteed in Scripture, Isaiah 58...

- ▶ Uncommon <u>Health</u> (Isaiah 58)
- ▶ Uncommon <u>Wisdom</u> For <u>Decision-Making</u> (Isaiah 58)
- ▶ Uncommon <u>Financial Favor</u> (Isaiah 58)
- ▶ Uncommon <u>Family Restoration</u> (Isaiah 58)

I would love to hear from you. Email me today at **DrMurdock@TheWisdomCenter.tv**..!

Your Faith Partner,

*Mike Murdock*

P.S. Will You Become My Ministry Partner In The Work of God?

PP-03

✂- - - - - - - - - - - - - - - - - - - - - - - - - - - - - - - - - - - - - - - - -

# It Could Happen To You!

## A Focused Seed For Daughter Unlocks Miracles..!

As I was praying, He said, "turn the tape on." Just as I did, you were telling the story of...And the exact words that I heard were, "plant a $58 Seed for..." That is the name of my daughter who knew the Lord, but at the time was not walking with the Lord the way she should. Needless to say, I planted a $58 Seed! Gradually...God turned her heart in a greater way toward Him. Thank you Jesus!

At the time I planted the Seed, she was in serious spiritual and financial trouble. Several years before, she had been in a car accident and the case had dragged on all of these years. She had "no hope" of receiving any settlement from the accident. She won a court case concerning an injury in that car accident and was awarded a large amount of money!

M. - AZ

## God Responds To 3 Seeds "Assigned" For Her 3 Children..!

In March of this year, I planted a $58 Seed for each of my 3 children. Right away I could see a move of God's hand on their lives.

Now, my two teenagers are involved in youth for the first time, my oldest has been filled with The Holy Spirit and doesn't want to miss church anymore. All 3 are going to a Christian School and loving it. It had not been my plan, nor can I afford to send them, but I believe the desire and drive was sowed in us the day I sowed the $58 Seeds for my children, to accomplish His will for their lives.

C. - KY

# It Could Happen

## Rent Paid For 6 Months..!

When I was at your meeting in Dallas, I planted a $58 Seed. In 58 days, I received a receipt stating that my rent was paid in full throughout the lease of 6 months. Looking forward to seeing you.

S. - OK

## Income Increases 100 Times The Size of $58..!

Over the last two years, God led both of us out of our full-time jobs. We attended the Sunday, February 14, service in which Mike Murdock ministered. In response to his message about the 58 blessings and the offering which was taken, we dedicated our offerings for our family and for our own financial assistance. Mike Murdock said that we would see the answer within 58 days. Monday night, God's answer came "suddenly." We received a surprise telephone call that offered...full-time work for a project through the end of the summer, the projected income is more than what we figured he would have to earn for us to be able to meet our needs for the entire year! By the end of the project, the income will be 100 times that of our offering. God is indeed good and really DOES multiply your Seed! Monday was Day 50 since Mike Murdock ministered and...starts work on Day 57!! Praise the Lord!

J. and C. - IL

## Unexpected $2,250..!

I mailed in $58 in April and unexpectedly got $2,250 for our ministry.

M. - VA

## 10 Year Battle With IRS Ends..!

We want to say that when I sowed the $58 Seed when you came to our church that week, a 10 year battle with the IRS that had put us out of business came to an end as we suddenly won our medical hardship case with enough of a refund to pay off our lawyer!

J. and R. - IL

## 100-Fold Return..!

I recently watched a replay of a telethon, you were talking of 58 blessings of God. The Holy Spirit moved on me to call. I had a stroke in April and was unable to use my left arm and had not worked since then. The next day, God sent a way to save my property. We also had a considerable amount of stock transferred to us; have started receiving Social Security for Disability after waiting 6 months. One blessing after another. The stock was exactly 100-fold!

T. - FL

## Debt Cancelled After $58 Seed..!

While you were with us...in Palm Springs, California, I sowed a Seed of $58 dollars to your ministry. One week later a debt that I owed of a thousand dollars was CANCELLED! My mother, who did not have $58 dollars at the time, gave $10. One week later she received a blessing of $5,100 and a nice increase in pay. I know that your ministry is true and God has called you to be a Financial Deliverer for many, including me.

J. - CA

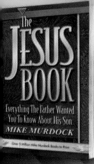

# Miracle 7
## BOOK PAK!

**DR. MIKE MURDOCK**

**Dream Seeds** (Book/B-11/106pg/$12)

**7 Hidden Keys to Favor** (Book/B-119/32pg/$7)

**Seeds of Wisdom on Miracles** (Book/B-15/32pg/$5)

**Seeds of Wisdom on Prayer** (Book/B-23/32pg/$5)

**The Jesus Book** (Book/B-27/166pg/$10)

**The Memory Bible on Miracles** (Book/B-208/32pg/$5)

**The Mentor's Manna on Attitude** (Book/B-58/32pg/$5)

The Wisdom Center
**Miracle 7 Book Pak!**
Only $**30** $49 Value
WBL-24
Wisdom Is The Principal Thing

Add 20% For S/H

Quantity Prices Available Upon Request

ach Wisdom Book may be purchased separately if so desired.

# Crisis 7 BOOK PAK!

**DR. MIKE MURDOCK**

❶ The Survival Bible (Book/B-29/248pg/$12)

❷ Wisdom For Crisis Times (Book/B-40/112pg/$9)

❸ Seeds of Wisdom on Motivating Yourself (Book/B-171/32pg/$5)

❹ Seeds of Wisdom on Overcoming (Book/B-17/32pg/$5)

❺ Seeds of Wisdom on Warfare (Book/B-19/32pg/$5)

❻ Battle Techniques For War Weary Saints (Book/B-07/32pg/$5)

❼ Seeds of Wisdom on Adversity (Book/B-21/32pg/$5)

The Wisdom Center
**Crisis 7 Book Pak!**
Only $30 $45 Value
WBL-25
Wisdom Is The Principal Thing

Add 20% For S/H

Quantity Prices Available Upon Request

*Each Wisdom Book may be purchased separately if so desired.

**THE WISDOM CENTER**
4051 Denton Highway • Fort Worth, TX 76117

1-817-759-BOOK
1-817-759-0300

─You Will Love Our Website...!─
MikeMurdockBooks.com

# Money 7 BOOK PAK!

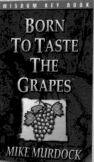

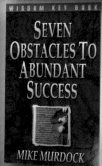

DR. MIKE MURDOCK

**❶ Secrets of the Richest Man Who Ever Lived** (Book/B-99/179pg/$15)

**❷ The Blessing Bible** (Book/B-28/252pg/$10)

**❸ Born To Taste The Grapes** (Book/B-65/32pg/$3)

**❹ Creating Tomorrow Through Seed-Faith** (Book/B-06/32pg/$5)

**❺ Seeds of Wisdom on Prosperity** (Book/B-22/32pg/$5)

**❻ Seven Obstacles To Abundant Success** (Book/B-64/32pg/$5)

**❼ Ten Lies Many People Believe About Money** (Book/B-04/32pg/$5)

The Wisdom Center
**Money 7 Book Pak!**
Only **$30** $48 Value
WBL-30
Wisdom Is The Principal Thing

*Each Wisdom Book may be purchased separately if so desired.*

Add 20% For S/H

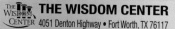
THE WISDOM CENTER
4051 Denton Highway • Fort Worth, TX 76117

1-817-759-BOOK
1-817-759-0300

*You Will Love Our Website...!*
MikeMurdockBooks.com

# Sampler Pak

## The Wisdom Papers of Mike Murdock

### *30 Different Wisdom Papers For Only $10..!*

7 Keys To Motivating Yourself! (WPMM#1PK)
7 Qualities of An Uncommon Leader (WPMM#2PK)
Guidance (WPMM#3PK)
When You're Tired of Waiting For A Miracle! (WPMM#4PK)
12 Facts You Should Know About Wisdom! (WPMM#5PK)
7 Things You Need To Know To Become A Millionaire (WPMM#6PK)
15 Facts About Miracles (WPMM#7PK)
20 Ways To Improve Your Relationships (WPMM#8PK)
The Master Key To Achieving Your Dream..! (WPMM#9PK)
Expectation (WPMM#10PK)
14 Keys To Managing Your Mind (WPMM#11PK)
Greatness...The Disguised Treasure (WPMM#12PK)
The Uncommon Dream (WPMM#13PK)
Nurture Relationships Connected To Your Dream (WPMM#14PK)
The Seed of Submission (WPMM#15PK)
Surviving Your Season of Testing (WPMM#16PK)
Unlock Your Miracle...For Your Uncommon Dream (WPMM#17PK)
Prosperity...And 3 Scriptural Reasons You Should Pursue It (WPMM#18PK)
Territorial Order (WPMM#19PK)
Loneliness, Love And The Christian Single (WPMM#20PK)
How To Delegate Effectively (WPMM#21PK)
Dealing With An Enemy...18 Facts You Must Never Forget..! (WPMM#22PK)
Peace Is Not The Absence of Conflict...It Is The Absence of Inner Conflict (WPMM#23PK)
Your Assignment Will Always Be To Someone Who Is Hurting (WPMM#24PK)
The Financial Crisis And The Believer (WPMM#25PK)
The Unhappy Voices Around You (WPMM#26PK)
Are You Nurturing A Strength or A Weakness? (WPMM#27PK)
10 Master Keys For Parents And Teachers (WPMM#28PK)
Passion: The Secret Weapon (WPMM#29PK)
Move Toward The Voice of The Holy Spirit..! (WPMM#30PK)

The Wisdom Center
**30** Titles
ONLY **$10..!**
add $2.00 S/H
WPMM 1-30 PK
*Wisdom Is The Principal Thing*

**THE WISDOM CENTER**
4051 Denton Highway • Fort Worth, TX 76117

**1-817-759-BOOK**
**1-817-759-0300**

*You Will Love Our Website...!*
**MikeMurdockBooks.com**

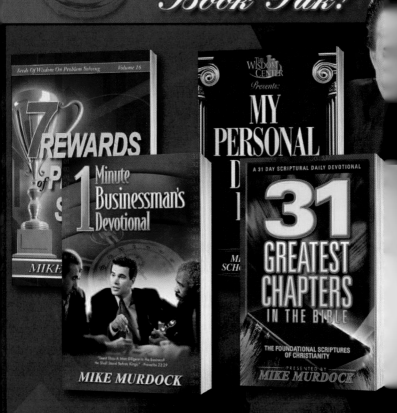

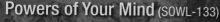

# Prosperity Secrets 4
## Book Pak!

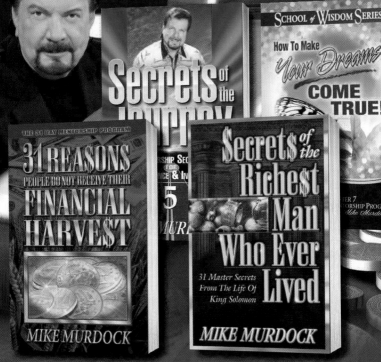

1. **Secrets of The Journey, Vol. 5** (Book /B-96/32pg/$5)

2. **How To Make Your Dreams Come True!** (Book/B-143/32pg/$7)

3. **31 Reasons People Do Not Receive Their Financial Harvest** (Book/B-82/252pg/$15)

4. **Secrets of the Richest Man Who Ever Lived** (Book /B-99/179pg/$15)

*Each Wisdom Book may be purchased separately if so desired.

The Wisdom Center
**Prosperity Secrets 4 Book Pak!**
Only **$20** $42 Value
PAK-28
Wisdom Is The Principal Thing

Add 20% For S/H

# THE TURNAROUND Collection

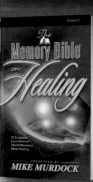

**❶ The Wisdom Commentary Vol. 1** (Book/B-136/256pg/52 Topics/$25)

**❷ Battle Techniques For War Weary Saints** (Book/B-07/32pg/$5)

**❸ Seeds of Wisdom on Overcoming** (Book/B-17/32pg/$5)

**❹ The Memory Bible on Healing** (Book/B-196/32pg/$5)

**❺ How To Turn Your Mistakes Into Miracles** (Book/B-56/32pg/$5)

**❻ 7 Keys To Turning Your Life Around** (DVD/MMPL-03D/$10)

**❼ The Sun Will Shine Again** (Music CD/MMML-01/$10)

*Each Wisdom Product may be purchased separately if so desired.*

The Wisdom Center
**The Turnaround Collection**
Only $**40** $65 Value
PAK-15
*Wisdom Is The Principal Thing*

Add 20% For S/H

 **THE WISDOM CENTER** 1-817-759-BOOK
4051 Denton Highway • Fort Worth, TX 76117  1-817-759-0300

*You Will Love Our Website...!*
**MikeMurdockBooks.com**

# CHAMPIONS 4
## *Book Pak!*

1 **Secrets of The Journey, Vol. 3** (Book/B-94/32pg/$5)

2 **How To Make Your Dreams Come True!** (Book/B-143/32pg/$7)

3 **Wisdom For Crisis Times**
(Book/B-40/112pg/$9)

4 **The Making of A Champion**
(Book/B-59/128pg/$10)

The Wisdom Center
**Champions 4
Book Pak!**
Only $20 $31 Value
PAK-23
*Wisdom Is The Principal Thing*

*Each Wisdom Book May Be Purchased Separately If So Desired.*

Add 20% For S/H

# THE WISDOM BIBLE

## Partnership Edition

## Over 120 Wisdom Study Guides Included Such As:

- ▶ 10 Qualities of Uncommon Achievers
- ▶ 18 Facts You Should Know About The Anointing
- ▶ 21 Facts To Help You Identify Those Assigned To You
- ▶ 31 Facts You Should Know About Your Assignment
- ▶ 8 Keys That Unlock Victory In Every Attack
- ▶ 22 Defense Techniques To Remember During Seasons of Personal Attack
- ▶ 20 Wisdom Keys And Techniques To Remember During An Uncommon Battle
- ▶ 11 Benefits You Can Expect From God
- ▶ 31 Facts You Should Know About Favor
- ▶ The Covenant of 58 Blessings
- ▶ 7 Keys To Receiving Your Miracle
- ▶ 16 Facts You Should Remember About Contentious People
- ▶ 5 Facts Solomon Taught About Contracts
- ▶ 7 Facts You Should Know About Conflict
- ▶ 6 Steps That Can Unlock Your Self-Confidence
- ▶ And Much More!

**Your Partnership makes such a difference in The Wisdom Center Outreach Ministries.** I wanted to place a Gift in your hand that could last a lifetime for you and your family...**The Wisdom Study Bible.**

**40 Years of Personal Notes...**this Partnership Edition Bible contains 160 pages of my Personal Study Notes...that could forever change your Bible Study of The Word of God. This **Partnership Edition...**is my personal **Gift of Appreciation** when you sow your Sponsorship Seed of $1,000 to help us complete The Prayer Center and TV Studio Complex. An Uncommon Seed Always Creates An Uncommon Harvest!

*Mike*

**Thank you from my heart for your Seed of Obedience (Luke 6:38).**

# This Gift of Appreciation Will Change Your Bible Study For The Rest of Your Life.

The Wisdom Bible

MY GIFT
C
Your Sp
of $1
Praye
Stud
Wisdom Is

# BATTLE
# 7 PAK

1 **Wisdom For Crisis Times** (Book/B-40/112pg/$9)
2 **Seeds of Wisdom on Overcoming** (Book/B-17/32pg/$5)
3 **Seeds of Wisdom on Warfare** (Book/B-19/32pg/$5)
4 **Seeds of Wisdom on Adversity** (Book/B-21/32pg/$5)
5 **Battle Techniques For War Weary Saints** (Book/B-07/32pg/$5)
6 **The Mentor's Manna on Adversity** (Book/B-81/32pg/$5)
7 **Seeds of Wisdom on Enemies** (Book/B-124/32pg/$5)

*Each Wisdom Book may be purchased separately if so desired.

THE WISDOM CENTER   1-817-759-BOOK
4051 Denton Highway • Fort Worth, TX 76117   1-817-759-0300

You Will Love Our Website...!
MikeMurdockBooks.com